Jon Schau

Jon´s Book 1

english

People seem to think it is so boring to be mediocre or normal.

At the same time, they are terrified of being seen as strange, different or abnormal.

PREFACE

Preface

In March -April 2004, I laid in a coma in the hospital for almost precisely 5 weeks. I went into a coma as a result of pancreatitis. Twice whilst I laid there, my brother was informed that it was over. That I was dead. And, while my family was distraught with sadness, I experienced the two most fantastic journeys I have ever been on. Here is what I experienced:

DYING

I was dead. Twice. Or at least, that was what the doctors called it.

On March 3, 2004 I was rushed to hospital in Bodø in Northern Norway. I had a very strong pain in my stomach, and I thought that I was to be given some pain-relief and then be sent home. Instead, without me knowing it, it was the start of the most fantastic journey in my life.

In a matter of minutes after arriving at the hospital, I found myself in Intensive Care. I asked one of the nurses:

"Is this not where you put people that are REALLY ill?" "Yes." "Then what am I doing here?" After a slight hesitation, she said: "We didn´t have anywhere else to put you right now."

That was the last thing I heard before waking up in another hospital, in Oslo, exactly five weeks later.

When I woke up from coma, my brother was beside my bed. He said: "This has been a very close call. Twice I was called up from the hospital, and they told me you were dead." I thought: "Wow! Was that what it was?! Was THAT being dead? I cannot wait to go back!"

And now I am going to tell you what made me think that. But first, the most important thing I will ever write:

What follows is NOT the truth. It is exactly how I experienced it, but that does not mean that it is True. I believe, as in every other aspect of life, that we all have our own unique perspective, which then again decides how we see reality. It looks different seen through different eyes. So, I choose to be honest INSTEAD of telling people what the Truth is. In reality, Truth and Honesty are actually complete opposites.

Ok. Now. Here is my experience of dying.

I went through four phases. The first phase, as I have come to see it afterwards, was about showing me that I was not here anymore. That I was on the "Other Side", that I was dead. And since I was never brought up in any particular Faith, there was no obvious image that could be held up before me to tell me that I was now in the "Afterlife". You could not use, say, Heaven or Hell, as it would not tell me that I was dead. Nor would any image of Nirvana, or any other religious perception of what "afterlife" looks like.

Instead, I was experiencing being killed over and over again. There were absolutely no pain involved, it was rather like a tiny annoyance. First, I was run over by a tram, or a streetcar. But somehow I managed to rewind the time thirty seconds or so. Then I ran into a dark alley. I stood there, believing that I had escaped, only to be stabbed in the back with a knife. I was a little annoyed, but I turned back the time again, and ran down the street instead. Suddenly I was shot in the face. Another small irritation, I rewinded again, and then I was run over by a car. I do not know for how long I tried to escape like this. But at one point, I was so fed up with all this running, so I just surrendered. "If I am supposed to die, let me just die, then."

The instant I felt that, there was a complete change of scenery. Everything turned completely dark. And then, in the distance, I saw this magnificent Light. It was bursting with life, with energy. And the feeling? Like being head over heels in love,times a thousand. I know it is impossible for anyone to get that, here. Since head over heels in love

3

is as far as we can imagine. But it still is a thousand times more. Since everything feels like that, is like that and there is so much of it that there is room for nothing else.

It is like a force in itself, not only something I can feel inside. It is outside, inside, everywhere. It is everything there is.

Suddenly I found myself traveling into this Light. Actually, I am not sure wether or not it was me who was moving, or the Light coming towards me. Anyhow, soon I was inside the Light.

Words are not anywhere close to being able to describe the feeling within this Light. It is pure Love. Nothing else. Like completeness. Like having become part of, and therefore built into perfection. As complete balance. It is the most incredible feeling *ever*. At the same time, *empty*.

Suddenly it struck me: "What have I agreed to now? Did I consent to Jon seizing to exist? Am I now part of something much bigger? I looked down, looking for my body.

I could still see it, but I could also see through it. And I see that this Light, which I am now dwelling in, is that which I AM MADE OF. The very thing, or substance, that I believe myself to be lacking whenever I think I am exhausted, or sick, I am now bathing in! It is AWESOME!

Then I start looking around me, since there is so much more Light than "me". "If I am this Light, then what is all the rest of it?" Then I see that this Light *consists of everyone*.

4

And this Light has sorted itself in such a way, that those other parts of the Light that I know best, is standing closest to me. My grandparents, all four of them. My mother, my father... And then, a huge surprise: I see my brother. «What is he doing here?! He is not dead?!?! He sits by the bed in the hospital!» A thought passed by; "Is there a part of us that is always HERE?" There was no answer, only the question.

THEN. The most extraordinary thing. My darkest secret. The very thing that I think I must forever hide from others, that worst thing I ever did. That exact thing...is what they show me... they want me to see that this is the part of me they LOVE THE MOST.

What kind of a place IS this?!

Please don´t try to grasp this with your thinking. FEEL it. Feel what it does. I am now at a place where words don´t exist. Try to be there with me: words do not exist. Then, try to think without words... It is impossible. Without language, you *can not think*. You can see images, and feel, but not think.

I start realizing exactly what place this is: It is *before judgment*. I find myself unable to do what I do all the time when on "this side": To judge. I cannot put labels on anything. Research shows that while here, in the physical, we spend on average 2,9 seconds to complete our judgment of people. Suddenly, here it cannot be done. I am unable to judge, to mean, to define. All I can do when meeting "others" here, is to become something else. Or not. I can not judge, I can only become more, or not become more.

So here, all that I am, is the one who is experiencing. I am what I feel, or *sense*. That is the part of me that is experiencing this. I am the one experiencing, that which is experienced, and the experience itself, at the same time. So to speak.

What I suddenly realize, or KNOW, is that this dark part of me is something I have invented. I am the one who have defined that part of me as being wrong. It is not like that here. To them, I have never done any evil. Nor good. Here are no definitions. I have done something. Said something. No definition. The defining is something we do here, in the physical world. It is an invention of our minds to be able to *understand* the world around us.

Then I realize what this means; I am exactly as I should be. There is nothing wrong with me. I was never a mistake. Nor was I ever right!

That insight qualifies me for the next phase, which you probably heard of before: Life passing in review.

It is not just passing by, like a train. It is much more like The Elections on CNN. As if there is a huge touchscreen which I control. I can go back and forth at my own pace. The film of my life. Remember, I am now not looking for errors, to see wether I did «good» or «bad». I am looking at my life to see *what happened*. What are my *experiences?* At that point I discovered something that has since become very important to me. My «film of experiences» was almost blank. I had actually misunderstood what it is to experience something. I had believed that seeing poor children in Africa on television is to experience it. But it is not even close.

What I have experienced, is what I have felt. What I have LIVED. Thinking about poor children is only turning poor children into a mindmade concept, which I then define and judge to be *wrong or right, good or bad.* That led me to believe having experienced it. But that is NOT having been there. And I realized that most of my "experiences" were actually just thinking about different concepts. So, that which in this review qualifies as an experience, is what I have grasped emotionally. Which has changed the very who that I say that I am.

Later, when I have spoken to audiences about this, people have asked me what I mean when I use the term "to have emotionally experienced something". An example: You are a football coach. You never won the championship. For twenty years you have asked other coaches: "How does it feel to win? What does it feel like?" Suddenly, you win. What has then happened? You are not asking anymore. Now people can come to you and ask how it feels. YOU have experienced it. You can emotionally go there. And in this context: It has happened. It is felt. It is caught on the tape.

Jon Schau

Then, when I feel that I have the overview; what are the experiences I bring with me, I enter into the last phase. Or, more precise, the last phase that I experienced. I do not know if there are more.

And that last phase is a place with a name. I know what it looks like. All the descriptions of the previous phases, are my tiny words trying to describe the indescribable. With this final phase, that is not the case.

This place is called The Core of Being. And it looks like the inside of an egg. More precise: It has no corners. It is earthly brown. And there are two doors. The one that I entered in through. And another one, exactly the same, across the room. On the outside of the door I came through, it says: Death. On the inside, Birth. On the inside of the other door, it says Birth. I do not know what that door says on the outside.

What happens here is very simple. I hear the question: "Do you want to continue, or do you want to go back?" To use the metaphor with the film again: I have very few images on my film. And here I am, at the photo store, being asked: "Should we develop the film?" To me, the answer was clear. «I have to go back».

Zap. I am back in the hospital bed.

This happened on a Tuesday. Two days later, on Thursday, it happened again. Exactly the same journey, with the exception of phase one. I did not need being

8

killed to surrender to dying again. So this time I went straight into the Light, and from there I knew where I was.

This story is not complete without something that happened two and a half years later, in 2006. I read a book, where the different phases was described stunningly similar to my experience. And, in that book, the last phase also has a name, and, would you believe, it was... The Core of Being. An amazing incident for me. That book was written by Neale Donald Walsch. I want to take this opportunity to recommend his books. They have meant the World to me when it comes to getting to grips with what happened, and to dare to be true to myself. This particular book is called Home with God.

And that is exactly what I think happened: I was invited to visit God. And it indeed felt like Home.

Kind regards,

Jon Schau

Jon Schau

PROLOGUE

What you are about to read is weird. Just so you know. It is for me, too. The first time it happened, which was a few months after I came home from the hospital, I didn't understand anything - except that it ended with some words on a sheet of paper. This is what I experienced the first time it happened:

Autumn 2004:

I had been working quite intensely for a while trying to find a topic – or at least a starting point for a topic – for my upcoming stage show. I sat with a notebook in the kitchen; it was around 3 am. Then it happened. I wrote:

Must decide on something. Idea as I write this:

All the subjects, topics are good, don't focus on the pain by omitting what you don't need. That which comes without effort, is what you will use. Everything that must be worked at/forced comes from another source.

So – just begin, and just see what comes easily to me?

Yes. Follow this, and not only the content, but also the form will create itself.

Strange to sit like this. It feels right, but at the same time, as if I'm a little crazy. Thinkink that I am someone...

Are you saying you are not someone?

No. But it feels a little like stealing. Stealing someone else's form, someone else's invention. (Not so long ago I had read Neale Donald Walsch's books «Conversations with God», which in terms of form, is exactly like what you are reading now.)

There is no discovery that is not mine. And you are part of me. Who do you think you are stealing from?

Okay, I get the point. But I can't get rid of the thought that if I show this to anyone, then I'm imagining it. I have read something and sit down and «steal the idea».

You're not writing books, are you? This is not written to be published. It is your tool.

I know that.

Then, what are you fussing about?

Will D (Jon's partner) think I've gone mad if I show her this?

Not at all. Your fear of appearing to be crazy is just that: Your fear. And your fear is not her fear.

Am I talking to myself now?

Am I talking to myself now?

Yes – in a way. We are all one.

Exactly. Do not be afraid of anything, Jon. Be without fear. That is the very point. Be without fear – because fear is what blocks the dialogue with your inner self.

I'm not going to show this to anyone but D...

No. It is not meant for others either.

Crazy...
(I sat looking out into space and waited for something more to come.)
Boy...it stopped.

'Crazy' is not a question...

Ha! This is fun!

I think so, too...

13

(I sat and tried to formulate something in my head...
Wanting to write, trying to think up something.)
That method was slightly wrong?

Don't think. It just blocks me out...

You answer a little too fast. I don't have time to write, I
am lagging behind.

I can see that. Better now?

Yes. It fits now.

Good.

Can't you say something really clever, something that I
couldn't have come up with myself?

There is nothing that you could not have come up with yourself.

Not very convincing?

*Jon, you are trying to convince yourself. Just stop doubting. As
long as you doubt, you cannot have faith. Either you have faith or you
doubt. You cannot keep both in your head at the same time.*

That was a little clever ... Now I have to go to sleep.
Goodnight! I sat and waited for an answer ... Nothing
more...
(Then I went to the toilet, and as I stood there, I thought:)
I feel a little crazy now..

That is how it feels to talk with me. You must let go and allow yourself to be a little «crazy».
Good night!

This has since continued. I have been doing this for 5 years now, writing this way, without thinking. Gradually, I started to write in English. I don't know why exactly, that's just the way it comes to me. I have even had to look up words in dictionaries afterwards to see what they actually mean.

It feels strange to share this. At the same time, it's just something I must do. One last thing, before taking the plunge: The first person in this book could be anyone. It is not I, not you. It is me. Living inside each and everyone of us.

I AM IMPORTANT

Don't underestimate yourself.

Who said that?

Me. Me. Me. (Many voices)

Is there like a whole gang up there?

Yes. And we are all with you in this. We are depending on you to not underestimate yourself. It is YOU and no one else who will do this. Who can do this. You must trust yourself, and you must trust what you receive. For there is no one else who gets exactly the same as you do. It depends on your "filter. You have heard that what comes from here, is distorted via the filter of the one who receives it. BUT – we also use it consciously. We make use of YOUR filter in order to get exactly this through. We need you to be focused. For this cannot

16

come through any other filter than you. Only you can do your part of the job. Do not place any limitations on yourself. Do the opposite. Everything you can imagine, you can also do. In reality you have no limits.

I feel really inspired now!

That s good to hear. Now listen carefully, because this is important: There will be periods during this process where you will not see where we are going. You will feel like you are completely lost. When that happens, I want you to remember this: TRUST ME! If you need to, write it in big letters on your notice board. You will at times have nothing left but your faith in me. Your trust will make all the difference.

I am not asking you to submit your will, or subdue yourself in any way. Ask questions, be critical, wonder – be curious, eager. It will keep you in the process. And that is where you have to be. Be on your toes, be open.

I think I'm ready.

Then this is our simple agreement: You trust me – I help you. It is through your faith that I speak. Without the faith, no process. Your faith is my mouthpiece.

Alright. I understand. I trust what I receive. And take it seriously. At the same time, it is important that I am both critical and curious after I have received it. Like a signal to you on what I need help with. Something like that?

Exactly. Precisely like that.

Do we need to have any specific work routines?

I think that café was good. Don't you agree?

Yes. It was very peaceful there.

Then that will be our routine. Go there every day. Your location is actually not so important, but you must sit alone, and you must set time aside for this. At least 1 hour each day. And begin meditating again. It is easier to get in connection with you then...

Okay. Meditation and at least one hour per day alone with you. Anything else?

Treat yourself to a decent pen. It is your most important tool. This one here has gotten far too sluggish. We are going to fill this book, so you need something proper to write with. But, again, focus on what is most important:
-Stay in the process. Don't allow it to come to a halt. You know how.
-Trust me.
-Don't underestimate yourself. You are made to do this. -Ask

questions about everything.
-Keep your eyes and ears open. Everything is for a reason.

I am looking forward to it.

We are too.

We'll talk tomorrow. Thank you for your help and for everything being as it is.

Yes. And- one more thing: Write from love, not out of irritation.

I love you.

(smile)

TRUTH

There is one subject I need to explore. The Truth. I seek the truth, but what is it? I guess that what I am saying is that since everyone have their own truth – what does it mean; to seek the truth?

That is a very good question. And you are completely right about the truth being dependent upon who sees it.

Yes, but how can I tell the truth – or even more complicated- how can I show the truth to others?

It is not possible to speak the truth. There are actually no words for it. And, if you think about it, how could it be possible? Since all people experience the truth in their own way, they would need their own words for it. Their own language, actually. A language nobody else would be able to understand.

Hmm. Interesting.

Yes, it is. As I said; it is a good question. But the fact that it is not possible to speak the truth does not mean that you cannot bring the truth to the world.

How?

By being the truth. Your own truth.

But will it mean anything for anyone then?

Much more than you will ever understand.

Hmm. How does it work?

Ok – I will try to explain. No person's truth is The Truth. The absolute truth is the sum of all truths out there.

I understand. Awesome! So what you are saying is that if everyone lives his/her own truth, we will be able to see the absolute truth?

Correct.

But it's not easy?

No, it is not easy. There are many more elements in this than just people. I can't go into it now. It isn't possible for you to understand it.

Ok, but back to what you said just before. How is it possible for me to bring truth to others?

By being your truth.

Is that all I can do? I mean- there has to be more than that?

Take a little time, right now, to contemplate what it means; "being your truth". It implies a lot more than what you first assume.

Like for example?

Such as seeing clearly, listening openly, speaking honestly. Imagine being honest about everything to everyone.

Oh... Yes, I can see that this could have some major implications...

You see, you cannot teach people what the truth is, but you can show an incredible amount of people where it can be found.

Yes – I can probably do that.

You will do that. Definitely.

Now, I have a question about methods. For example, I understand that telling people what they are doing wrong is a bad method. Correct?

Yes – because you don't know if what they are doing is right or wrong. No one knows that. Except themselves.

You re saying that I don't know what's right or wrong, but still I know if they are honest with themselves – isn't that right?

Yes.

How do I know if people are honest?

You already know the answer to that. You pick out these people all the time. With great ease. It is just that you think that they are mistaken, when what they are doing is being dishonest about themselves. That is two different things.

Because?

Because it is entirely possible that they are honest with themselves, while you think they are mistaken. It is not a given that people will change what they do, even if they are fully aware of what they are doing. The difference cannot necessary be seen from the outside, even if this change in focus has taken place. This change is internal and consists in the person having gone from being an unconscious victim of life to being conscious in his/her choice of how he/ she experience life. From powerless participant to creative director of experiences.

So what you are telling me is that I can help people become aware of themselves, but whether they are or not cannot be assessed on the basis of their actions?

Exactly! Now you hit the nail on the head!

Okay – now I understand. I think.

You do. I am happy for you.

Me, too. Thank you. I think that this has been a very good conversation.

If you say so, it is so.

I mean it.

I know.

CREATION IS CONSTANT AND
INFINITE

I am thinking that if there are no absolute truths, then there are no absolute un-truths? That everything that is not true, can become so?

Of course. There are no truths / anything right, and there are no un- truths / anything wrong.

Hm. Pretty amazing, but I can see that it is so.

Yes. I know you can see. You have known this all along. But now – start using it. Being it.

I will. Can I ask you one more thing?

Of course you can.

Some talk about spiritual levels, that there are 7. Deepak Chopra, for instance, writes about this. He says that Jesus and Buddha were on level no. 6. Do you agree?

They were where you are. But that was another time, another setting. So you must relate to the world around you. Just as they did. But you can do the same as they did, and more. Or not. It is up to you. You decide.

Can I do as they did?

Yes. You will do as they did. BUT IN ANOTHER WAY. In a 21st Century way, and it is very different. You will therefore choose completely different expressions, which, by the way, they would have done if they were here now. Or are here.

Are? What do you mean? Are they here now?

Think. I have told you before: There are no limitations as to what you can do. NONE. Do what you think best.

I'm getting such a feeling of ego-intervention here now. Can I really think that thought at all?

Of course you can. And don't imagine that the two you have mentioned here didn't have the same thoughts. I promise you they had a lot of them.

Okay. I believe you, but feel extremely humbled at the same time.

So did they. I'm telling you: You can change the world. You will change the world. But remember that there are many of you. Anyone can choose to be one. And as for your humility: It is in a way «seared» into the insight you have. You could not have been where you are without that humility.

No. I understand that. Because I couldn't see it in myself if I don't see the same in everyone else at the same time. It's quite ingenious, this universe of yours!

Hehe. I agree.

Awesome! It's a very positive spiral, this. Because when I see the connection, I also see that we are all part of the same, and therefore all equally important. We have the same value in our joint project. All of us. And therefore, it isn't possible for me to «take off» from what you are telling me now either. If I take off on my own and see myself as something more, something greater than before, I will also automatically see it in others.

Exactly. Now you've got it.

I love you. Thank you for everything you share with me and all of us. Hope I can live up to this task.

You can. And you will.

Yes. I cannot do anything else. Not now.
—

Today, I have discovered something exciting: We create, right?

Yes.

Jon Schau

But we don't create with thoughts. Not with what we think of as thoughts. We create with the underlying thought - if you understand what I mean?

Of course I understand. And you are not completely off the mark. The underlying thought, as you call it, I think I will rename that to "your experience". Your experience is what is manifested. Your experience is what is created. So, if you think about becoming, let s say, enlightened (whatever that is)- then ask youself- why? What is the experience you have now, that wants this something else? You will probably find that your experience is that you ARE NOT. And that is what is created. So it is more about why you want it, than what you want. "I want a car" means "I do not have a car". If your experience is that you do not have a car, then it is. So- if what you are after is a car, then START EXPERIENCING IT. Only thinking about it, will create the opposite.

But is it correct then, as I believe, that it is not desirable to control my own thoughts, but instead focus on where they originate from? If you originate from the essence of yourself, then everything is created just as an expression of love?

That's correct.

So I can safely assert that if I am afraid of going crazy – if I think about it often – then it doesn't help to take «control» by trying not to think it? It is a much better, more enduring solution, to do the opposite: Throw myself into being crazy, to then experience that I do not have it in me?

28

That is correct. Never place restraints on anything. Be who you are now. Then the «real» you will emerge more clearly, and the «artificial» will be lost, peeled off little by little. It is actually the case that if you live out all the things you are now, you will arrive more quickly at the essence. You will find nothing but who you really are.

And so on. Obviously. It's nice to have time to sit like this. I really value these tiny chit-chats we have now. It helps me focus. To centre myself.

I know that. You know that. You notice in our conversations now that it is the same whoever says what? I could play your role and you could play mine.

Yes. That's what I mean by tiny chit-chats. I have it all in my head, but it gives me a sense of something firm and tangible when I write it down.

I know. I like it, too.

Is there anything you can tell me about where to look? Anything I should pay attention to?

You are becoming more and more observant. You are becoming more and more certain. And you are looking in the right direction. If there is one thing I could need to remind you of, it is this: Remember that it never ends. There is always more. All «topics» are always in a process of change. At no point in time you will come to «now I know it all». Because then it will all stop.

29

Yes. And we don't want that. However, there probably isn't any danger of that. I *love* the process, and miss it when I'm out of it a little. Still, I appreciate your reminding me of it. Because I know how important it is.

Anything else?

No. I don't think so. I will just sit and be still for a little while on my own now. Just Be.

May it do you much good.

SEEK AND YOU SHALL FIND

Everything you see, everything that is, are cells in my body. I love them all, and therefore give them everything they need to be happy. Each cell is just as important to me. None are overlooked, none ignored. Can you say the same about the cells in your body?

The pains in your chest are a way for the cells to let you know what they don't want. You give them something they ask to avoid. You must do a little detective work to find out what it is.

A little secret: To love yourself is to love all your cells. When you love yourself, you love your WHOLE self. And it has a little to do with what you have read about loving your «bad» sides. Love your illness, for it is also part of you.

People are saved by feeling your love. Is it a bit like that with me and my cells as well then?

What do you think?

31

Jon Schau

I think it is.

The whole universe is built up in the same way. Look outwards and upwards with a telescope, or look down through a microscope and you will see the same. It is the same order, or disorder if you will, which lies behind everything. You can therefore learn much about yourself by looking at what's around you. Observe. Seek and you will find.

To me, this is a very interesting conversation. Not least because I already thought like this when I was much younger.

In many ways, you were more in contact with the universe then than you are now.

I know. And it is very helpful that I have been there. That I was once on a quest, or maybe even *this* quest. I found something new all the time back then. So I only need to remember.

Also, this might be a confirmation that we human beings often see concrete truths symbolically when it's really meant literally. Exactly this was, as I have understood it, Jesus' greatest frustration? That they perceived his message as something with symbolic significance, when it was actually meant quite literally?

Well, it was probably something he had great difficulty getting people to see. They didn't see themselves in him, and after all, it was that which was his whole point. «Look at me. I am the son of God. See what I can do. Everything I can do, you can do, too... Here and now!» But the people thought that it was something they could achieve like an award after «death», if they did life "right". It was (and is) a great misunderstanding.

Pity.

Or not.

Yes. Or not. Thanks for sharing this with me. Or thank you for making it available.

Thank you. It is your choice, all of it. What you choose to see, you see. What you want to understand, you understand.

I still want to thank you.

Who in the very end, is YOU.

Yes. And thank you for that!

You are in a grateful mood today?

Yes. I have much to be thankful for.

You do. And – think about it – you have created it all yourself. Continue doing it. Create. You
are the creator in your own high self. You are my creator.

See you at the café in the morning. We have a job to do.

Yes. We have. See you later.

Should I prepare anything?

Yes. Meditate before you go to the café. Come with silence.

Ok.

DON'T WORK. BE.

I'm ready then. Or no... I sit down and let my thoughts wander, then we'll see what happens.

Don't try. Just let it flow freely. Don't add expectations. Expectations create pressure. Here, there is no pressure. If just one word comes out of it, then it is enough. Don't prejudge how much is to be done before it is «work». Take the time you need. Don't «work». Be. Here.

Understood.

Good. For it is not a matter of you being ready or not ready. You are – just stop thinking about it.

This helps me. When you say that, everything loosens up.

You are in process now. This process will be different from what you are used to. It is driven by your joy – no pain, no compulsion. If

35

you feel any of that, then put your pen down and come back to the joy. Then you can continue.

Ok. (......long pause......) I feel that it's difficult to begin. Because there's, like, nothing I'm wondering about. I think so, anyway. So I don't need any answers, and so I don't get any either. If you understand?

I understand. Then consider this: Waiting is more than half of the process. Wait. But do it actively. Sit ready to write as you are doing now. Don't wait for «inspiration». Sit ready and wait. In the process. Do you understand?

Yes. I could not have translated it into words unless I did not...

Okay. Patient in the process. You often do not have patience. Do this therefore for at least 1 hour. You must be in the process at least one hour each day. Much of this work we are doing requires insight. And insight requires calmness. Which, with you, takes time. Creativity is not in the work, but in the break. A carpenter thinks about what he will make when he is not carpentering. When the thinking/break is over, he carries out what he has thought of. The breaks are my tools.

This process has no efficiency requirements. This process has is about maturing. And in your world, to mature is the same as to wait. Externally. Internally, it is something completely different. Therefore don't be occupied with what others may think about it. For them it looks like you are waiting. Only you will notice that you are maturing. But be very strict about keeping the two apart. Maturing is to wait- in process. To wait is only that.

Here, now is maturing. Here, now is in the process. Here, now is insight.
Here, now is not *to wait. Everything else is to wait.*

WHAT YOU UNDERSTAND, IS TRUE

I have noticed that people often claim that "some things never change". But that which they say is unchangeable, IS changing. Christianity has always found its answers in the same book. But the answers have changed. They change their interpretation of the book according to what suits them. Nevertheless, they refer to it as the eternal truth. Which truth in that book can they point to and say «It has been, is and always will be true»?

The answer is none.

Exactly. Because it is interpreted.

Exactly.

What you interpret for yourself, becomes your truth. It does not mean that your interpretation is true for anyone else.

Truth and understanding are closely connected. What you don't understand, cannot be true for you.

That is actually very deep... I think that is where the need for religion comes from: People want to feel secure. If you believe you understand everything, that feels secure, even if the sense of security is false. But for he who believes in it, it is still the truth, because it is all he understands.

You follow me surprisingly easily now.

You make it simple for me.

These are in no way simple thoughts.

What you understand, feels simple.

And that is why it is easy for Christians to believe in Christianity.

Are you now saying that to change the truth – if that is the aim – it can be worth it to consider doing so by using understanding?

It is often easier to get people to understand than to get them to sacrifice their truth. Yes.

Hmm. Amazing.

Do you think so?

Yes. Or actually, it is obvious. But I haven't seen that connection before.

You have understood it. And that's why it becomes evident. Or true.

You're clever.

You, too.

It strikes me now that laughter is a great confirmation of understanding. You cannot laugh at something you don't understand.

And so ...?

If they laugh at my description of the truth, have they also understood it?

Everything they laugh at, they have also understood. In other words – if they laugh, they say that what you say is within their vision.

Is that so? After all, they can laugh at the fact that I'm completely wrong.

If you are completely wrong, they don't laugh. Then they leave.

I see. I do not doubt you are right... I just have a slight problem absorbing it. It feels like
there's a flaw in the logic here...

You haven't understood it. That's why it isn't true for you.

Or I have understood it, and a little more...

And you have understood one more thing: When you understand more, you are able to abandon your old truth without any problems.

Now I must honestly admit that things are going a bit fast for me here. I understand what you say, but can't manage to think in order to check if I can logically agree.

And before you logically agree, is it not true for you.

Exactly.

Okay. Short summary:
What you don't understand, cannot be true for you.
When you understand more, you are able to abandon your old truth – with joy, in fact. Tempo is an important factor.
All three of these points are very important to our work.

I will remember that. I just have to think it through. I must understand it before it becomes true, you know! He, he.

He, he.

You understood. You laughed.

BE IN THE PROCESS

Awake at half past six - so wonderful! I wonder if there is a special reason that I wake up so early?
  Are you there?

Yes.

Is there something you want to say?

Keep your eyes and ears open this week. Be in process. It is very important this week. There are things that needs to be experienced.

Ok. Should I get up this early every day?

You control that yourself. But be sure to stay in the process. The important thing is that you are here, now. Just be here, present. Awake.

It strikes me – now that there are two children visiting here – that maybe it has to do with that? To learn from how they are in the process all the time?

It is not especially about the children. You could learn about being in the process every time you are in contact with children. Grab the opportunity that is there. You could do that all the time. You see, even in choosing the words grab the opportunity, *you imply that opportunity is something that comes occasionally and is quite rare. I am telling you:* There is always an opportunity, and it is never accidental.

That was a good way of describing process, I think. Hmmm.

Ask yourself that question all the time: What is here, now? How did I create this?

Is that the most important now – to be in the process?

I have told you before. That which comes easily to you, you use. Everything else is from another source.

So I don't need to «produce» text?

No. Not at all. Your feelings are absolutely right: You just stay in this process, whatever it is. That is what you need now. Writing is the easy part. And again – I have said it before: This is about maturing. Not a «work process». Give in to the flow. When you think that you must write, or produce, it just draws you away from here.

Jon Schau

It pops up in my head now: «I never sent you anything but angels»?

And that is also not accidental- that it pops up right now. Remember that all situations are can show you something. It is never created by chance. Regardless of which situation you are in, you have CREATED IT YOURSELF. So- what is it that you want to show yourself? That is ALWAYS the question.

Can you give me a hint about what to look for this week?

No. Because it is not my creation, it is yours. It depends on what you want to experience. And it is important to differentiate between experience and learning. Because, as I have also said before, there is nothing to learn. What you are looking for is your experience. And what you are looking to experience you will attract to you. It is not at all accidental. Not even the combination of people around you. Seek and you shall find.

Can you give me something to go by...?

Yes. I shall give you the truth. You have everything in you. Everything! Isn't that fantastic? You need no one apart from yourself, for in you, there is everything. Look within. All the answers are there. All of them. In the entire universe. You seek confirmation and learning, knowledge outside yourself. But everything is within you. You make yourself uncertain and insecure in this way. You don't need to!
Even this conversation is from inside of you. But because you yourself can't see how great, how infinite you are, you search outside yourself in the form of a chat with me. You never need to do

44

that. *I am in you. You are God. Understand that, and I never need to give you anything again! There you have my gift.*

Oh!

Yes. Oh! Do you remember the sentence you suddenly heard: Don't underestimate yourself...? Well, DON'T do it. You are everything.

This is very inspiring. At the same time, it's really hard to *believe*. Really, *really* believe. I understand what you're saying, and believe you. Still, it is very difficult to believe in it. Do you understand?

Yes. This is so strange with you human beings. It is the easiest thing in the world to make you feel small or even smaller than small. Someone say one sentence, and you think you are small. But when someone tells you how great you are, how important you are, you cannot believe it. Even if that is actually the truth! You easily buy into a lie, but find yourself unable to get the truth. You are one strange species!

Yes...But also, we are pretty great?

Touché.

I think I want to start the day like this more often. Talking to you makes me so happy and excited!

I am glad. Come here whenever you want.

Even if there is nowhere to come. For real. After all, I am just here.

Exactly.

Is there anything even greater behind it all? Something even greater than...

No.

The topics are clear?

Yes.

There is nothing greater than everything, perhaps? The truth. No, this is just plain horseshit. Now I'm writing just for the sake of writing.

Exactly. You do that. Do you see now how it is not about producing?

I get that. Smart way of showing me. Thank you.

My pleasure.

ABOUT MY HEALTH

Can you give me a hint about the chest pains?

I give you hints all the time.

About what?

Listen to your body. It tells you all the time.

Can you say something more concrete, or is there a point in itself that I figure this out on my own?

You already know that. Make a list of where and when they show up.

They come when I think about them. Waiting for them – I'm afraid that they will come right now.

Do you see how they come from your thoughts?

Yes...

Do you notice how the pains often start in another place, then move to the chest?

Yes. It is like I move them there. For it is there that I am afraid of feeling them. I have pain, and focus on the chest, and then they, like, move there.

Your father died of heart failure, didn't he?

Yes.

And since then you have had pains in the chest...

So the fear arose then, and so I somehow move them to wherever I am afraid of feeling them?

Yes.

Hm – the past experienced in the present. Because I am not fully here and now, I bring the past - and the fear also brings the future – into the present. If I am just here – now, then I do not feel the pain?

The pain is not here-now.

Good point. Very good point.

It is, isn't it?

So it's not about snuff then?

Certainly not. It has to do with you deciding that something is a problem. And then, to make it real, or as obvious as you need them to be, you recreate them as pains in the chest.

Thank you. This helps me.

Hope so.

I have read a little about diabetes today, and it seems to be a much more serious illness than I thought. I'm a little worried. Would I be able to do anything about it?

It is vital to listen to your body. LISTEN to it. It tells you everything you need to know. You should read up on it – just to know what you are dealing with here.

Would I be able to cure myself?

Everything can be cured. Everything is already cured.

So can I stop taking insulin and just take it for granted that it's gone, and then it is?

In theory, yes. But do you think you can do it?

Honestly - No. Not deep down inside. Not now.

*Well – no theories will ever be of any help. You must be patient with this, it takes time like
everything else.*

But, strictly speaking, there is no time?

49

No. But you make it. So that you can experience life. It is like a film. You are not able to see the entire film immediately. Even if every moment of it is already on the DVD. All events- one on top of the other. Everything at once.

I honestly think that this conversation is really dull. I'm getting nothing out of it. Nothing concrete that I feel I can use, anyway. I'm getting a little tired of it actually.

Okay. Let me then say this: The cure comes when you are ready. But you are still not ready. So the answer you are looking for is: Do what you can based on whatever you see now. Always do that. Keep yourself on track. Be in the process. It is like you are on a train to recovery. By and by, a station you come to will be the cure. Ok?

Yes. But I would rather have it now.

Why?

Because it worries me. It takes focus.

So don't let it worry you any more.

And how am I supposed to do that?

I have just told you that you are already on the train to recovery. The train just hasn't arrived at that particular station yet. If you have faith in me, it should make this relatively easy for you. Stop creating worry around this. Worry is not, now. Worry is something you add. Look past it. You are practically on your way to the doctor already.

50

I understand. If I just stick to the process, then everything will be fine?

Yes.

And that's it?

Yes. Don't add worry. It is not real. You seem to think that worry is something that comes from whatever it is that you experience. It does not. You add that. Sometimes it is helping you, sometimes it is not. This is an example of when it will not.

Ok, I won't add it, then.

Why are you a little grumpy now?

It is boring on this train.

If you look at the floor, yes. But not if you look out of the window.

You know, sometimes I hate the slowness of this process...

When you come here again, you will miss that slowness. For it gives you the opportunity to experience everything. What is it that you want? That which you want to experience, you will experience. There are many here who miss exactly that. You don`t need to spend any time being tired of anything. You can experience whatever you want – right now!

Jon Schau

Okay. I see that I'm fortunate. Quite a paradox, that. You all see me and want to be here. I see you and want to be there. Is one never content being where one is?

You decide that yourself. Right now, you choose not to be content with something that can *happen. It's not happening now, but you would rather invest your experience in something that could happen. It* might *happen. From here, that seems meaningless. Do you have any worries right now?*

No. I don't. Point taken. I see where you want to go. Here-now. Ouff! I'm tired of that, too. It is like it s the same answer to everything! Here-now.

Have you tried here-now?

No, maybe not...

Try it. I promise that your frustrations will disappear. Because they don't exist. And that is why I repeat this "here-now" all the time. If you are here-now, then none of the things that worry you exist.

Ok.

Good.

Aha! Now I understood! By getting irritated by the fact that it isn't here now, I strengthen that it is not in reality ...

You do. And that's the way it is with many things. I tell you: WHAT YOU BELIEVE YOU ARE, YOU ARE. WHAT

52

YOU BELIEVE YOU HAVE, YOU HAVE. That's how easy it is. You just don't see it. The present moment - the NOW - is EXACTLY THE WAY YOU WANT IT TO BE! And that is actually something that I can't get involved in. For it is YOU who CREATE this. Not me.

Okay. So something came out of this conversation after all. I'm satisfied. I have seen more. And at the same time I knew it all along. These conversations are crazy!

Replace the word conversation with journey.

Okay. No longer crazy. Is that what you want me to say?

Well. I don't want anything.

No. And it is not always so easy to understand. Actually GRASP.

It took you six minutes.

I always loose, don't I?

You never loose, I think?

The discussion, I mean.

Me, too. You are discussing with yourself.

Yes. Do you now understand what I mean by crazy conversations?

Jon Schau

I always understand what you mean.

I am tired now. Good night.

Good night.

YOU ARE WHAT YOU THINK YOU ARE

I was very inspired by this Abraham channelling I heard on a CD
  the other day. Everything was so simple.

For most people, it will seem very advanced.

For sure. But only because they believe they are something else. When they see who they really are, it will become incredibly simple.

Yes. It is as I have always said. Change what/who you think you are, and EVERYTHING changes. For you ARE what you BELIEVE you are. That is, after all, what BELIEF really is: If you BELIEVE in miracles, you CREATE miracles. If you believe that you are healthy, then you are healthy. If you believe that you are rich, then you are rich.

I know that now. The connection has become very clear to me. I consciously create a great deal now, and there is more to come! I've really acquired a taste for it.

55

Jon Schau

READING ECKHART TOLLE'S THE POWER OF NOW

I just have to say that this book is completely fantastic. I get really excited when I read it, and it's about so much that you have told me before.

That book has been waiting for you. I am happy that you have finally found it. You still can't imagine how great influence it will have on you. This book will provide you with much important insight.

I'm so happy I found it. Like, to the core. Why, do you think?

It has been the intention all along. But you were not ready before now. He is so clear that you can look at it like talking directly to me. And with me.

I felt that. How will I find my mission in life? What the guru talked about as being «very important», and all that? You understand that I'm excited?

I understand. It is just that you are actually right in the middle of it. Do what you are already doing. Be in the now. The important thing is not anything you do, but the consequence of what you do. It is a very important thing to remember: It is not you, as in your ego, that is important. It is what you will give to others by doing this that is important. I don't mean important for you and your personal development. That will take care of itself. I mean for the universe. For life itself. And everyone who is a part of it.

So there's really no point in finding out why, I guess. It is again about the good old stay in motion, be in process, aware in the now?

Exactly. Exactly. It is throwing away time and energy trying to find out why. Do. Be. It is what you create out of being you that is important.

I like this. I actually like it very much. The idea of making myself, my ego, unimportant, presses all my buttons. I just dig it!

If you think about it, you have always known it is like this. You are here to do something for everyone else. And therefore also for yourself. And the universe. For me.

I work for God?

To the highest degree.

I feel somewhat touched now.

Me, too. It is easy to be touched when we are as in love as we are now. We are here-now. It's good, isn't it?

Good-y!

He, he.

What about the guru saying it had to do with music and film – doesn t it seem a little far-fetched?

Not at all! Go into yourself. Don't you feel it? This will be your way. I will reveal one thing to you: You are THE GREAT COMMUNICATOR. You can communicate with people telepathically, with body language, words, music, film. Whatever. You can and will do all of this. For you are me. Personified. In the physical dimension.

But everyone is, aren't they?

Yes. But not many are aware of it. And among those who are, you are the one who is meant to communicate this. Dare to think that thought. Get used to think big, then bigger. Think until you get giddy. And when you get there, you will be able to see the start of who you really are.

It baffles me that I don't feel this as a burden at all. It is almost embarrassing to say so, but I know ...:) I know that it's true.

From now on, turn your focus inward. It is there you will find the connection with everything. I promise you one thing: no matter how lofty your thoughts, it is alright. You are not equipped to think bigger

59

than what you are able to carry out. If you can think it, you can do it.

Thank you. I am so unbelievably thankful.

And remember- I am with you. ALWAYS.

YOUR POWER IS LIMITLESS

I would just like to say that I wonder a little as to whom it is I am talking to these days. It's such a gentle tone.

That is a very complicated question.

Because?

Because when all is said and done, there is only one. But still it is not. The best answer I can give is that the source is the same. Gabriel, Raphael, Anna, Dora, you, trees, fungus – They are all The Same. In another way, not the same.

It is God wearing several hats?

Yes – in the very end. In the whole and full truth, yes.

What then is the point with, say, angels?

Yes, I wonder. You tell me. You have created them.

Jon Schau

We?

I don't create. YOU create. I am. What you create, IS me. You must erase the image of an old man with a white beard. That is NOT me. I am inside of you. AND OUTSIDE.

Then give me another image, please?

Okay. I can try! Think of matter and anti-matter. That is ever-changing. Ever re-created. Not from itself, but from that which they consist of. And therefore, still from themselves. That's me.

I think I get that. All and nothing. As we have discussed many times before. Why am I unable to change the image of you as an old man, then?

Because you don't see your own greatness. You don't dare to see that you are me. You therefore create images of me as something other than you. But I am not something other than you. Even though I am also that.

Tell me more, please. This feels so good.

Very well. The greatest obstacle you humans have created for yourselves, is your highly developed ability to underestimate yourselves.

What is then held back by this obstacle?

The seeing of the great connection. The remembering of who you are.

And why is that so important?

It is not important at all.

What? You're loosing me now...

What is it you don t understand?

I don't know. Isn't that odd? When everything is not important, then... It is just incomprehensible that there isn't any point, any goal.

Well, that isn't completely true. Since there is not ONE goal, you conclude that there are none? Is that your logic? Well, there is a third possibility: There are MANY. That is the genius of all of this: You get to set the goals. Or not, if you don't want to. Total freedom. No less.

Could you say some more about this? I don t quite get it?

You often have an image in you head: Your own body as your own universe. Let's use that. Can any of the cells in your body do anything you don't want them to do?

Yes.

Okay then. What?

Grow into cancer, for example.

Jon Schau

Why?

The gods only know.

Yes, because you don't love yourself. You don't love your own universe.

I think that's taking it a little far...

Is it?

Where are you going with this? I really don't understand anything.

You don't love that cell that grows into a cancer cell.

How can you say that?

Because otherwise, there would be no cancer.

So all those who die of cancer wants to? Is that what you are saying?

No. I am saying that they don't LOVE themselves.

But, I love myself.

The cell which develops into cancer, too?

Yes.

After it has become sick?

64

Well, maybe not... So- you re saying that if I love myself, my cancer as well, then I won't get cancer?

No, you won't.

Hard to believe.

And right there, we are back to the same place again. Why is it so difficult for you all to believe?

I don't know.

Because you think that to believe is to believe in something other than yourself. You think that it is outside yourself. You think that you can be inflicted by something. I'm telling you: You cannot! You can create something. Yourself. I have said that you are me.

But I don't understand how you can do that - love everything and everyone in that way?

Because you believe that to love is something you do. It is not so. To love is something you ARE. This is the result of being everything.

And how do you keep yourself in this state?

I don't. I AM this state. Love is everything. Love is what I am.

I understand. Actually. But the question was about total freedom, etc.?

To love is to give total freedom.

Okay. I must reread this conversation again in the morning. It's a little «fuzzy» to me.

How?

I don't think I liked that example with cancer. I think perhaps it's a little nasty? I really don't know how I feel. Sounds like something I would not say.

It is because you see death as something other than what it is. You see it as something bad. When you see the whole picture, you will see that there is nothing bad about «dying».

Like I didn't want to see anything bad in that cancer cell?

Yes. You judge things. Stop that. It's completely unnecessary. Had you seen the whole picture, you would have seen that cancer is created, how, and that there is nothing bad or wrong with it. On the contrary, it can be the whole POINT.

Aha. It's not up to me to judge if that cancer cell is right or wrong, nor if it is good or bad to get cancer, or to die of cancer?

As I would have said it myself. Or as I said myself. Through you. There is nothing to gain by judging something or someone.

Yes, in fact. One thing.

What?

Laughter. I can make people laugh if I judge a fish and say that it is stupid.

And what is laughter?

Amusement. Fun. Extends life.

What extends life?

A good laugh.

Is it a good laugh to judge a fish?

Now you're asking me to judge.

Yes.

Okay. Yes – I think it can be a good laugh.

What is a bad laugh then?

No...I don't know. To laugh at others? Laugh at sick people?

Can you really judge if a laugh is good or not?

Hey, don't take things out of context.

Context? What context?

The context of the laugh. What is it about and what are the motives for saying it.

Are you aware that you are really, really out there?

Yes, I'm defining myself bigger and bigger. It gets more and more unclear.

So you can't even judge what is your own job? Not objectively?

No. I can't.

Okay. So − that judgement − you gained nothing by it?

No, nothing but spend time on something that ended up being nothing.

What with the laughter then?

Yes...?

You said you create laughs by judging animals?

Yes.

Are you sure that it is the judgement that people laugh about?

No − now I feel like a fool.

Why?

Because you pick apart everything I say.

Remember that I am you. So this is you picking apart everything you say.

Even more of a fool.

Why do you suddenly judge yourself now?

Damn. Am I painting myself into a corner here?

Don't know – are you?

To be honest, I lost my train of thought a long time ago. I can't even remember what we were talking about.

We're talking about you having nothing to gain by judging things.

Okay – Is that it? Yes... I'm completely confused now. My brain is boiling. I'm sweating, in fact.

Is that what you have to gain by judging laughter?

Okay. You're clever. Always right. You're faultless. I bow down to you and lick your boots. Satisfied?

Not completely – who is it you bow to?

You – Almighty smart-ass.

Me? Who I have said is ... ?

Jon Schau

I am the same as you.

So the Almighty smart-ass is you?

Me. Now it has become a good conversation...

Hard to please.

Bundle of fun.

Good assessment.
I just have to complete the picture a bit. There are some clarifications that are important here. What we have talked about here are absolute truths. From the Earth, they will appear completely wrong in many ways. There are so many factors that come into play that it becomes meaningless to try and understand it through earthly eyes. For example, when I say that you all create, "you" does not only indicate human beings. There are others. Many others. And many of them create much more consciously than you. So you must not think it as me saying that everything is created by humans the earth. Everything is created by me. By something that I contain, that I am. I promise you – there is much more than the planet Tellus. Remember this when we talk about absolute truths. It is important to keep that perspective.

I understand. And I believe I sense what you mean. It's absurd to only take into consideration what you call «you humans». It would be giving humans too much power, too much responsibility.

Yes – and yet, no. These are complicated things, Jon. We will never get to the end of this. There is ALWAYS more. And that is

70

perhaps all you need to know. There is always more. If you know that, you are always in the process. And that's where you should be.

I understand. Still, I know that I don't. But I understand enough to resign myself to the fact that I understand. I understand you. Yes and no. So yes, I know. Only, I have no idea.

TRUSTING IN ONESELF

You just said something very interesting.

Yes. It is time you began to trust yourself. You read books – which is good, of course, – I just want to talk a little about why you read. You often read books to find confirmation. You need confirmation that what you think you understand is really true. And you get this when you read that others have experienced the same things.

What you do not see is that this is a way to not trust yourself and your own experience. You do not allow yourself to believe in yourself until you get confirmation from others who experience the same things. That is not necessary. You know all you need to know. It's time to put this behind you so that you can contribute with what you are. Because – as you know – you can't be anything else.

Don't I need to seek in other places?

That is not what I am saying. It is always good to read and reflect on the experiences of others. But at the same time, it is important to understand that what brings you to where you want to get to, is not the experiences of others. It is your experience that is the key to becoming more, Jon. You have a tendency to trust more in others than in yourself.

Do I?

Paulo Coelho knows more than you, does he not? Neale Donald Walsch? Deepak Chopra?

Yes.

NO. THEY DON'T. There is no one other than you to ask about you, your abilities or what you are here to do. Never forget that. It is good to read books. But what will start your creative process is your faith in yourself. And when it comes to the subject of Jon Schau, there are no authorities other than Jon Schau.

Yes – I can agree with that. Thank you.

You're welcome. The final piece of the puzzle you find within yourself. You must make the decision to trust your own experience. When you do that, you are here. At the end of the tunnel. Briefly.

Thank you. I love you.

Thank you. I love you.

<Break>

What do I need to know?

Nothing. What you need, is to do.

Do what?

Turn back the clock on your lifestyle. Get back to where you were in Spain. And the important part, is that you start meditating again. It is nearly impossible to see the eternity if you don't. That is where you experience it. Within. Where there is silence. And that is important for you to do now. Because you NEED that. You need to feel it, not just know it.

I see. I will get to it right away...

Good.

TO SEEK IS TO FIND NOTHING

I know that «to seek» is to keep oneself in process. And when I find answers, I only discover new questions. I find this quite demotivating sometimes. In a way, it feels a little meaningless to seek something you never find.

You misunderstand. There is nothing to find. You are searching for nothing. And that is why you never find it.

I am looking for nothing? You make me crazy sometimes. Do you know that?

I don't make you anything. If there is anyone making you crazy, it is you.

Ok. I'll try to stay with you on this. So, what you're saying is that I never stop seeking. And when I seek, I find nothing. Don't you agree that this is a little strange...?

I'm sorry, but no. I cannot agree with that.

Why not?

Because the point of seeking is not to find anything.

It is not?!?

No – the point of seeking is to seek. Seek, find, and then continue to seek. For what you have found also changes the instant you find it. Thus it seizes to exists at the very same moment you find it. If you could find what you searched for, then it would mean that life is a constant thing. Life is nowhere even close. Life is creation. Life is unstoppable. Always in flux.

So it isn't the seeking that is important, but the creating?

Yes, but if you are to create, then you must seek. Or – not entirely. But to create something new requires that you seek. To seek is not to search for anything special. It is to find nothing, and out of this nothing, create something. To seek means to look for something new so that you can create it. If the search had anything to do with finding something, the whole process would have stopped. The universe would not be living. And that cannot happen. Never. Life is infinite. Life is all there is.

I actually understand this. Incredibly enough. What I need to ask then is why this that you describe feels so futile? I mean- to search forever is kind of pointless?

Why does it feel pointless? Why do you believe it is necessary to know everything? Why do you require that things die?

I don't know.

Because you look for security. And if you know it all, then you would feel secure. Would you not?

Yes, I would think so.

Okay. So let us stop the universe right now. And then you study it until you know it all.

Yes.

Yes. Then what?

Eh.... Not much, I guess.

I don't think so either. I think it will be the same as with many «religious» people. Since they have a book with all the answers, they stop searching. They go to church every Sunday to tell themselves that it still applies, what they already knew last Sunday.

Hehe... Yes.

Does it seem appealing to you?

Not very, no.

Can you then explain why it is so bad for you to keep searching?

Okay. I admire Jesus. I admire Buddha. I admire those who had the ability to see everything clearly. Those who actually understood how the universe works.

They did not.

What?

They did not understand it. What they understood was that it cannot be understood. And so they let it be. They observed and learnt how to create more consciously. But nobody can understand this completely. They understood that they did not understand.

But their understanding was, of course, what made them so special. If not, they would have been completely ordinary people.

They were completely ordinary people. But they did not see people as ordinary. They saw people as the miracles they are. As the Gods they are. Creators of the universe.

This is so strange. Sorry about the language – but what the hell is it that I'm looking for?

Nothing. Look for whatever you want. Create what you wish to find. This is what free will means. What else could it be? To have the right to see and understand something that has already been made by someone else, and then be critical about it? To point out things someone else has forgotten to create or has not thought of? Don't you think it is better to be a part of the whole creation process? To see what you don't like, so that you can recreate it, instead of just thinking about changing it? What if you had spent your life constantly raising your hand and say what you thought was a pity that no one else thought of? I think it would bore the life out of you.

I agree! But what am I here to do?

Yes, what can that be? Could it be whatever you want to do? *Would*
that be uncomfortable for you?

It would be incredible!

Which I have said many, many times that it IS. But – and this is
what I find so remarkable – you, almost all of you, choose not to
believe me. In your minds, this is too good to be true. «ME? Do I
actually mean anything? Am I not a little, defective creature who
should say «I am sorry» every single time I do something «wrong» or
«crazy»? Could it actually be true that I am fantastic?» For one
reason or another, you have always chosen to say «NO». What Jesus
and the other «ordinary people» did was to say«YES» to that. It is
also all you need to do. Say «YES, I am fantastic».

This is almost beyond belief!!

Why am I not surprised?

SPIRITUAL AWAKENING

Gradually during this process, I have thought that I would have saved a lot of time and energy if I had been given this insight much earlier. You know, this "awakening", why did it happen so late? Why did it not happen on the day I was 25 for example?

You are turning this upside down.

Could you be so good as to explain why?

It was not the spiritual awakening that took time. It was arranging a major crisis in your life that took time. And everything that you needed to experience before the crisis has given you the result that you yourself have created.

Which is?

A massive awakening. Major insights. Many insights. The whole picture. You wanted to see the whole picture, nothing less – and it took time.

Which, of course, is not time at all, but rather a number of situations from which to gain experience. Such as here, on the physical plane, is translated in time.

You have started to get good at describing this now.

Thank you. And I agree. I feel really good now. I feel real.

You are in contact with reality.

Yes – I believe I am.

YOU ARE RESPONSIBLE FOR WHAT YOU CREATE

(I sat on a bus and a ferry, and had this magnificent feeling of oneness with everyone present. It was as if I could see through everything. Hear their thoughts, see their lives.)

That was quite an experience today, that feeling of unity. On the bus and on the ferry. But one thing surprised me a little – why was I afraid?

Yes, why?

Because I had the feeling of being alive, truly alive?

Is that what you think?

I don't know. That is what I'm asking you about.

You ask me what you think?

Not exactly. I'm asking why I was afraid.

And I asked: What do you think?

Yes. Are you leading to something here?

What you saw was that you are yourself responsible for what you create. You are responsible for how you see the world. And it was unpleasant. You saw your own greatness. You saw that you are me. And it made you think of things you are not used to thinking.

Yes. Please go on...

It is usually not easy for human beings to see their own greatness. Because it shows them what responsibility they have. It is not easy to take yourselves seriously. You see, before you arrive at this point, you do not take full responsibility for your own life. And as soon as you reach this point, it is an end to the excuses. There is no one else to blame for anything. The illusions have gone, and you see the world through my eyes.

I can understand that it got me feeling uncomfortable...

There is nothing strange about it. It is actually the most common reaction. When you reach that point, real barriers are broken down.

But there's even more, I feel? Lurking in the background is a feeling of unease.

Yes. There is no way back.

Oh. Frightening...

So decide something else. When you see the truth, as you have done today, it becomes clear to you that there is nothing else to do other than to live what you are.

Yes – I felt that. I was a little afraid of what I might say during the interview just afterwards.

Again, there is nothing unusual or wrong with that. This is just like your previous breakthrough – it takes some time to adapt. Then you are back in the comfort zone again.

I'm almost there already.

Yes, I know. Do we agree then that this is not something to worry about? When you think about it, nothing has actually changed. Reality is the same, even if you have seen more of it. Most human beings do not see what you have seen during their time on earth. They see it only when they come here.

But at the same time – I still haven't seen anything?

I think this is your most important character trait, Jon - that you never stop. Never.

Stay in the process, yes? When you think you know it all, the process stops.

Yes, you have a special ability to be on the move regardless. There is no doubt about that. Maybe you could think of a way focus your use of it. What are you looking to experience?

I want to turn it into something I am, so that I live the truth, and not only know about the truth. I think...

I don't have any doubt that it is exactly what you will do.

I suddenly get this feeling that you are a little proud of me. And as I am saying that, it strikes me that I might come across as I'm fishing for compliments, but I'm just honest. It's how I feel right now.

You are absolutely right. I am proud of you. When you are proud of you, I am.

Yes, I'm aware of this – deep down, that is why I'm here. To let you experience being yourself – through me... So now you know how it feels to be proud.

That's right ...

Is this a state of mind I need to be in all the time?

There is nothing you need to do. Everything is up to you. Go there when you need it, or when you want to.

Jesus. Was he in that state all the time?

No. Again, there is no need for that. I actually think that you will find that sometimes it is not really useful. Sometimes you will need to be present in the physical reality with all of your awareness. If your head floats around up here all the time, I believe you would quickly seem completely distant to people. You need to have your feet firmly planted on the ground just as much as you do here. It is incredibly important that you find a balance that suits you.

Ok. Do I need to be there when I'm on stage?

Not at all. Come in before you go on stage. Come here to prepare. When you are on stage, you need to focus all your attention on that.

I know that the same moment you say it. Of course it's like that.
There is another thing I would like to ask you about. Will I be able to heal myself soon?

All you have to do is do it.

This is strange. Suddenly, I wonder if I really need it...

It is absolutely not strange at all. You needed your illness. It has taken you all the way down to zero and then built you up again. Of course you doubt if you are ready. I tell you; as long as you have this doubt, you will continue to need the illness. When you are completely certain that you do not need it any more, it will be gone.

I understand. Thanks so much for talking to me. You are a great support for me. To be honest, I don't know what I would have done without you...

Do you not know? Go back 5 years then...

No thanks. I am not going anywhere!

Good for you. I love you.

I love you, too. Goodnight.

FED-UP WITH SPIRITUAL GROWTH

Right now, I'm irritated, restless, irritable, indisposed, dissatisfied. It feels as if everything has reached a deadlock. Everything is standing still. It feels as if there is a storm coming. That I am close to a breakthrough of some sort. The feeling of being very close to something. Something is about to happen, but I don't know what.

I am tired of all the theorists in the spiritual universe, tired of «guessing» all the time. I want to arrive. Now. Pardon the expression, but the one that best describes me now is: What the hell is the point of all this? When I'm as I am now, Dora is affected by it. I am curt, impudent and reserved. I don't want to be, but that's just how it is right now. I'm tired of searching. There is no process. Standstill. Dead. As boring as hell.

And yes, I know I can do something about it myself. Go out and think up something. But I feel pain and anxiety as soon as I put my snout out of the door. Why can't something, just something, a little thing – come for free, come easily? In that respect, this universe is poorly made – it sucks. If there is a meaning, a task I am meant to do, say, stand of my head, or what the hell, why not just give me a bloody clue? This isn't so goddamn easy.

Sitting there like a gang of spectators looking on. "Let him find it himself"... Molasses. M o l a s s e s! That's what that method leads to. It s sure as hell not strange that things are going slowly down here with the spiritual growth and everything when you all with the answers sit there like poker players holding your cards so close to your chest! Don't hold the rope so tight, damn it! Don't let me do everything alone! You must see how I twist and turn, search under every stone? What is the point of the silence?

You don't want to be where others are. You want to go farther. Will go farther. You want to lead the way. You must therefore stop comparing yourself to others. You send such strong signals that you want to go on. You have even defined where you want to go. Still, you want your process to be like everyone else s. No process is similar. You are attracted to going to another level. Then other things are required.

Okay. What then?

More discipline. Being more on the alert. More scrupulous. You must let go more. You think, why do I have to give up snuff to be healthy, when loads of sportsmen who use snuff are in top physically shape? You don't train like them. You neglect your meditation. You neglect your food. And none of this is wrong. It is just that this is not leading you where you want to be.

You must decide, Jon. If you want to get there, you must go that way. And I know that that is what you want. Stop complaining. It is you who wants to go there!

I just think it's difficult to go 100% for something that feels so vague.

Okay. It is your choice.

I need a little understanding here. A little consolation, maybe?

You don't need any of those things. You go the way you point out yourself. Therefore comfort is way off what you need. You do not comfort someone for getting exactly what they ask for, do you? Do you give someone a Christmas present and then comfort them for it? That is what you need to see: What you think you need comfort for is a whole drove of Christmas presents from here. A constant stream, actually. And they are all exactly what you 're asking for.

But I don't ask for pain. Fear. Do I?

You only get what you ask for.

I understand that I attract what I am afraid of and all that. So that I will be able to choose something else instead. I just can't see how I choose it. I think I am choosing something else.

You knew it yesterday.

That I find assurance and security in being sick? No demands, etc....

In that sense, yes.

So I need to be sick until I get well?

Now you have it.

Hmm... it's actually dawning on me now, yes. I, my higher self, knows that I need to be sick. Because the moment I am healthy, it is when I have to be healthy...? I will be healthy when I need to be. When I need to work. But until then, it is better for me to be sick...?

Yes, because you cannot work and do what you must do until you are well, so you must be sick until then. Isn't it obvious?

Yes. Strangely enough.

Jon. It is the fact that you are sick that has given you the opportunity to do/be what you do/are now. Without the illness, you would have been half drunk in Volda or some other place. With the illness, you are where you are now. *In Spain. With Dora. With a child on the way. Without alcohol. With this awakening. With great ideas for a new ground-breaking show. It is the illness that has been the backdrop for being able to give you all this.*

Ingenious!

Jon Schau

I think that you can advantageously say that the illness is not just pains in the chest? It's nothing to speak of if you weigh it up against the positive sides.

Yes. That's so. And I therefore embrace the illness. For the time being. Until I am healthy.

Exactly.

Thank you. For the -enth time. You're great!

They say so. Have a good time with your thoughts.

ENLIGHTENMENT

After reading that magazine I wonder: Where am I going? What am I aiming for? Enlightenment?

What is enlightenment?

Exactly. What is it?

It is ever changing. You can be there, but never get there.

Go on...

Enlightenment is not a place. Enlightenment is nothing permanent. It moves. As life does, it changes all the time. You can be enlightened, but as soon as you see yourself as that; being THERE, you are not enlightened anymore. It is like a train. You can get on it, but as soon as you think your journey has ended, and leave the train, you're no longer a traveller.

I understand. And to me it is very clear. Easy to see what you mean.

Jon Schau

Yes. I know.

Has anyone ever been able to BE enlightened?

There are two answers to that. Yes and no. And they are both right. It is like this: You see everything and at that point you are at an enlightened state. But if you do not keep the process running, you are not there anymore.

Enlightenment has to do with understanding life. And life is me. And I am always changing. So you will have to keep searching FOREVER to STAY enlightened.

So, what you say, is that if I – right now – could see everything Jesus saw, I would not be enlightened? Because life in itself has changed, so his understanding of life would today, be inadequate?

Yes. Of course. If Jesus came back right now, having stopped his process when he was Jesus, he would be just as out-of-date as the churches that say they represent him.

So, maybe the most important feature in anyone being, at least from time to time, enlightened – is to stay in the process? Because yesterday's experiences are already outdated tomorrow?

No. They are outdated TODAY.

Yes. But the rest of it would be true?

94

Yes. It would. Haven't you noticed that in yourself? Jon – you are an enlightened human being.

Sometimes. Then you take some "time off", a vacation in a way, before you "tune back in. That is how this is.

You're saying there is no such thing as a permanently enlightened being?

Not on earth. If you were in an enlightened state of mind all the time, you would leave the earth.

Would I?

Of course. Life as you know it – the physical world – is an ILLUSION. As soon as you see though the illusion ALL THE TIME what would you see?

Nothing.

Well, not quite. But the physical world would not exist for you anymore. It would INSTANTLY vanish before your eyes.

Hmm. This is intriguing.. I mean, I am striving towards enlightenment, but actually, on the level of the soul, I don't really want that. That is what you're saying, right?

As long as you still have a purpose in life, that would not be in your interest, would it?

No... I guess not...?

You guess? Surely you can do more than that?

Well, in my mind, what we have been talking about here, means that it must be so?

Right.

I am often right nowadays, am I not?

Of course you are. Right now, you are in a state of enlightenment. And you go there frequently. When you need to. At the same time you KNOW that you need to stay in the illusion to get where you want.

I like this conversation. It is the most rewarding in a very long time.

Well. You've been on and off the train. And when you're off, having a break, the level of conversation is decided by that.

I'm not in the mood, so to speak?

You might say that.. Remember, there are no absolute truths. There is no end of this railroad. And that is the whole POINT OF IT!!

Yes. Of course. Or else YOU would not be enlightened, even. Because YOUR process would stop.

YES! And that is impossible. Life cannot stop. It does not have a choice on that. It can change shape, but it can never NOT BE.

I know this. But the perspective you are drawing in this conversation, I find very exciting and new (to me, at least..). I love it, actually. Because that means this can never be boring, like school. When you know all there is to know, all there is to know changes. I love this!

I know you do. That is why you are where you are. In and out of enlightenment.

So what I said to D earlier, about giving lectures about how to be enlightened, is not possible. Because when you decide on the curriculum, you GET OFF THE TRAIN!?

Exactly! Very good! You really have it now!

Yes. I really do, don't I? At least until I think I do...

You have come far, my son. You have come a FAR way.

I am proud.

So am I.

Thank you.

Thank you for listening.

ABOUT DEFINITIONS

Free yourself of definitions? Is that what you are saying?

Yes. Don't define everyone you see. It keeps the brain preoccupied with very insignificant things.

Yes. Now that you say it, I see that it does.

Yes. You see, in the beginning you did not do this. You could see someone, and say: "That person is." Then you started to act as if there is a blank spot after that sentence, which you have to fill in: "That person is ...bad", for instance. You do not have to do that all the time. It is as if a great deal of human brainpower is being used to solve some kind of crossword puzzle or something.

I see. Maybe I should not let others define me either then?

No. Of course not. You must have noticed how strong that resistance is in you? The resentment you have of being defined? Do you know what that really is?

Yes. The answer has come to me already.

Ok. Then write it down.

When I'm defined, I am nothing.

Exactly. And that is why you should not define others. It is making people invisible to each other.

FREE YOURSELF FROM
EXPECTATIONS

Take away expectations, and the judging of situations disappear. And when that is out of your life, so is your fear of life. Every situation is just as it is, if you don't compare it to anything. If every moment is let to be just that – what it is – you will have peace in your heart.

People have been so caught up in the illusion of separation, that they have become addicted to comparison. They compare themselves with others. They compare their things and the things of others. They compare their thoughts with those of others. They compare their life to that of others. People even compare the situations and moments in their lives to what they have expected that moment or situation to be.

Can't you see how much grief and sorrow and pain you afflict upon yourself by doing that? Don't you see that that is really what creates your so-called problems?

I say to you: Rid yourself of expectation. Rid yourself of comparison. Then you will be able to see how perfect life really is.

100

And if you look at the moment you are in RIGHT NOW, don't you see how perfect it is showing this to you? You see – what you see now, is what you have wanted to see. *That was what you ordered. Once you see that, your troubles are gone. Because then you just order something else.*

Think about what you did in Croatia. You did not expect anything. You did not, therefore, compare it to anything. And you were able to see the perfection of the moment.
Do the same thing now. See the perfection of it. And ALL is well.
There is one other thing I want to tell you about. Responsibility.

Most people feel that taking responsibility for something is the same as taking the blame for something.
They think that when you say that they are responsible for their own lives, you tell them that they should blame themselves for their own misery.

That is not even close to reality. It is only when you see that you are responsible for your own life, to be able to see what it is all about. To see every moment for what it is.
You see, people tend to blame everything "bad" in their lives on others. When you do that, you say that it was created by someone else. It makes you unable to look inside yourself to see why the situation appeared in the first place.

When you take responsibility for your own life, you proclaim to the universe that YOU are the creator of your life. Which is the reality of everything.
And as the creator, you can look upon the creation and understand it. You can figure it out, by asking yourself. "How did I create this? What did I make visible for me to see?"

There is ALWAYS an answer to that question. And when you find the answer, you move on to the next thing you want to create.

If you do not take responsibility for your life, you will be creating the same situation over and over again. And you will continue to blame others for what is happening to you.

That is the real Catch 22 of life. Blame it on others, and you will continue to do so. Take responsibility, and you will grow.

THE MESSIAH

Excuse me- did you just say "You must allow your greatness to be"?

I most certainly did. You must allow your greatness to be. Because if you don't see your greatness, you could end up believing in someone else. You would be amazed if you knew how many that actually to that.

Most people think that they have chosen their beliefs freely. It is not so. If they take a closer look, they will see that it has been chosen for them.

And since they don't see the Greatness in themselves, they feel that it is not up to them to change what "someone great" did.

I tell you: If you don't see that you re every bit as great as anyone who ever lived, YOU ARE AT FAULT. You are everything Jesus ever was. Buddha. Gandhi. Take your pick.

I cannot see the logic in what you are saying. I don t get the point.

Jon Schau

Oh, yes you can! And you do!

Yes, I do! And it feels GREAT! The conversations we have these days are just...WOOW!

I told you you were ready now.

Yes. Thank you so much.

Now I will tell you the truth about the Messiah. You see, there is some confusion surrounding that. People tend to think that Jesus was the Messiah. But he was not. As the same time as he was.

You see, the Messiah is ALL OF YOU. You carry the Messiah inside. Every single one of you.
That is what Jesus saw. And that is how he created miracles. He spoke to the Messiah in every one he spoke to.

And he tried as hard as he could to tell you this. He sacrificed himself to show you that you can do the same. Because there is nothing to be lost. Ever. Nothing is ever lost.
So Jesus was the Messiah, as are all of you. Do you now see how great you are?

(Loooooong break.)

I needed a break. Sorry I was gone for a little while there. You were talking about the Messiah. Can you say something more about it?

People are like candles. Unlit candles. Jesus came to show happens when you light that candle.

But people misunderstood him completely. They saw it as if him having the candle, was what made him great. But the greatness in him, was that he had it lit. *That candle is in every human being. And that candle, when lit, is the Messiah.*

Jesus was trying to spread the flame, the light?

Exactly. He hoped that the flame from his candle, would spread, and light all the candles. It did not happen.

Unfortunately.

Why judge? Maybe the flame is still strong enough to spread? You can help accomplish that. Because you have the same flame. Go spread it.

I most certainly will try to do that. In my own way.

That is the only way. For you. That is what we're trying to achieve here. That everyone become his own way.

You never know which flame will start a fire.

Well said. And it is spot on describing our "tactics". There are more candles burning on Earth right now than ever before – put together.

Put together?!

Yes. There are many.

I think I know about a few...

Of course. When you know what to look for, it is easy to spot them.

Anything else before I go to bed?

No. Time is not important anymore. We can speak anytime – anywhere. If you are tired, you should go to sleep. And then we pick up where we left off next time.

Ok - good night, then.

Good night it is.

ON MEANING AND PURPOSE, CONVERSATION 1

What are we doing here? Why am I here? What is behind everything? The search for meaning and purpose has preoccupied human beings since the beginning of time. Many have wanted to own the answer to this question, and every time someone think they found it, the answer is changed or adjusted - adapted to the times we live in, and somehow, always in accordance with the goals of the power structures of the time being.

As an example, reincarnation was taken out of the Bible in the year 324 AD. I guess someone realized that people would be more likely to follow the instructions of the elite if they were to believe they would face Judgement Day when they died.

I want to explore my purpose, your purpose, our purpose, the earth's and the universe's purpose. I want to know the answer to everything. Everything cannot hold nothing, but nothing contains everything. So, what I want, is to know the answer to Nothing – which in my understanding is the true Unlimited.

Ok - now I'm excited. What is it I am here to experience? What is the purpose?

Well – your particular situation is special. As is everyone s.

Your specific task is to become a way to make it easier for others to achieve spiritual awakening. You are on earth to "loosen the cork". You are here to create circumstances so that people can access their own spirituality more easily.

Yes - I understand. And my illness was perfect for creating such circumstances. I hope I'm not on the wrong track when I say that for me it seems really obvious as to why "circumstances" were such that Jesus was born in a stable and that he had low social status. He would not have been able to do what he did if he'd been born a King.

To me, this is a good sign that you are on the right track for learning more about who you really are. You would not have seen this if you did not have a clear understanding of it.

I think you're smart. Really smart. Because now I see that I couldn't take anything away from my life. Every single detail and event has a meaning. Because all of them together have created the person I am today. Perfect.

Yes – it is, isn't it?

Yes—I should say so. I'm so happy now.

I know – I also feel it.

One more question. I'm a bit surprised that you answered my question so unambiguously. After all, you've avoided answering this question before.

No – I haven't. It is you who have been avoiding it.

Me? Why?

Because you were not ready.

Does that mean I'm ready now?

Yes. You cannot see anything that you are not ready to see.

—

Conversation 2

Stupid question maybe, but what are we doing here? Why do we humans exist? What is the purpose?

Nothing. Nothing is your purpose. And I mean this in two different ways. Nothing, like emptiness. The reason for this is that it does not work with anything else. It must be empty for you to fill it with what you want. Take some time and think about how it would have been if there was an answer to your question. There wouldn't be any point in living.

Yes. I see! Strange – if life had a point, then it would be meaningless.

I understand what you are saying. You use the word meaningless. That is your choice. Strange, mysterious, forever incomprehensible. Call it what you will. The point is that life would not have a meaning if there was a meaning. Think about sex. If it wasn't a mystery to you, then you would lose interest. The point of sex is that it feels good. You don't know why it feels good, and you don't care. Because it feels good, you carry on with it. Life is like that. It is supposed to feel good. There is nothing beyond that. As long as life feels good, you carry on with it. There is no why.

I like this. Really!

I know you do. But do you know why?

No.

You see? It feels good. And you don't know why...

I love this!

Yes, and that is strange to you.

Yes, it is strange to me.

It has to be like that. Life without mystery about life, would ruin life itself. It would be meaningless if it had a meaning.

Wow. Really – Wow! But you talked about "nothing" having two different meanings? What's the other one?

Split the word in two.

No thing.

That's right. Life is no thing.

Meaning?

Life is no thing that you can be successful at, nor fail at. Life is either the ever present, ever growing experience of which you are aware, or it is made to be a thing created by your judgment.

Say again? About the latter part?

When you judge, Everything turns into Your Meaning About Everything. It is not as it is anymore. It becomes something that only exists in your mind. Your life turns into a mental construction, rather than just being Life itself.

CONVERSATION WITH JESUS

Hello. I want to talk to Jesus. Is that possible?

Of course it is. He's here for you. Just as I am. Ask away.

Ok. Jesus, are you there?

I am, my dear friend.

I know it is you. You always give me this feeling of calm. Of love, I guess.

I am glad you can feel that. Thank you.

You are thanking me? Well, I guess that is a lot less weird than it would be one year ago.

We talked a little last year as well. What is it you want to talk about?

Actually, I needed to FEEL you. It has been so long. I missed that feeling. But now that I have you here; I am afraid I might be coming on too strong. TV, the new show and everything.

I think you are doing great. You have only good intentions with everything you do. And that is what counts.

Did you ever have that feeling?

All the time. And it is necessary to have that feeling. But your love for God – meaning all people, all of humanity- will always win. Love conquers fear. Every time. The fear helps you build more faith. It also reminds you to stay connected, to take time to have conversations like this.

When were you afraid?

Most of the time.

Most of the time?

Yes. And that helped me a lot.

How do you mean?

It showed me where I needed to direct the light. Whatever you fear most, is where you have to direct your love. Because, once you love something, fear disappears automatically.

So whenever I feel fear, I direct my love in that direction, and the fear is gone?

113

Exactly. There were so many times I needed to feel fear to know where to direct my loving attention.

You know, you're a genius. This is amazing, and it s like I KNOW it to be true.

Because you are a genius. Do not trust what you have been taught. Stay focused on universal knowledge, and you will do works of genius.

Is this where this Christian dogma came from? About staying on the right path?

Yes. It has, as have a lot of things I said and did, been slightly misunderstood. I never implied any kind of punishment for doing "wrong" things. It simply meant, that if you are consistent in doing things for the right reasons, you cannot not succeed. It was never meant to scare people into living a certain way. It was meant to make people follow their hearts instead of their fear. Because no act out of fear will ever bring anything good. And certainly not what it is that you think you want.
You see, any wish you make out of fear, is really not what you wish for. It is turning everything upside down.

The church is good at that.

As they were two thousand years ago.

I want to ask you; the Bible we read today - does that describe what really happened? Or has anything been added or subtracted from it?

114

It has been edited.

Really?

Oh, yes. Several times. When you read the Bible, you will see that a lot of things in it is built upon fear. All of that is false. It is either a misunderstanding, or – in many cases – pure EDITING to give certain people power over others. It really does not take much thinking to figure out which is what. You can just feel in your heart what is true, and what is not. At the same time – it is BASED on the truth.

I see. So turning water into wine, feeding lots of people with just a few fish – that is true?

Yes. That really happened. And do you know what? You can do the same. Whenever you believe you can. I could not do ANYTHING that you cannot also do. Right now.

I guess this is why I find it so easy to love you. You just showed us our own greatness. You never tried to be the greatest human being of all times.

Well, that is correct. I always told people that they could do the same as I did. I even said they could do more. But no one even dared to think it.

And that had a lot to do with people's fear. A fear very often imposed on people by the Church.

Correct.

Are you saying here that you, Jesus, don't like the Church?

No. I don't dislike anything. I am saying the Church is more about people, than it is about God. Because in the Church, they think they know WHO God is, not even seeing that WHAT God is, is NOT a WHO. Thing is, they have never even asked themselves that question. Not with an open mind. Not with the desire to see what it really is.

Wow, *that's* an eye-opener. Really!

Yes. I think it is.

You know; You are amazing. You have this ability to tell the most complicated things in a way that is so easy to understand.

No. Not so. I am using YOUR ability to do that. You do that better than me. And that actually has a lot to do with the society around you. Nowadays, you can use a lot more tools to get the point through. In my time, those possibilities were very limited. The image that people had about God, was very limiting.

So you're saying we have a golden possibility to get the message through now?

Of course.

I'll think about that. A lot, I think.

I know you will.

I am very tired now. Thank you for all you have done, and continue to do.

I am glad I can be of assistance.

I love you.

Me too. Love you.

YOUR DOUBT IS YOUR FAITH

Never underestimate your self or your experiences. You create a block when you doubt. Doubt breeds doubt and nothing else. If you want to believe, then decide to believe.

Believe in everything you experience. Then you will also discover that faith breeds faith. Choose faith. You have faith in what you believe in. And by having faith, you open yourself up to more faith. The only limits are those limits that you set yourself. YOU ARE WHAT YOU BELIEVE YOU ARE. When you doubt, then remember that the doubt is the reverse of faith. See doubt as a limited part of your faith.

Define everything as faith, and you will find that you have faith. You see, faith and doubt balance each other out. One explains the other. Therefore, you cannot believe without doubting. But you can tell yourself that doubt is really also faith. And then faith and doubt pull in the same direction. Doubt becomes a confirmation of your faith. That is what it really is.

If you do this — value your doubt as an important part of your faith — they confirm each other rather than balance each other out. You will find that the journey to your faith will be at least twice as fast. Your doubt is your faith. Your friend.

THOUGHTS ORDER RESULTS

Try not to think too much. It creates a block. I notice that you are thinking.

Ok?

When you think, you think about what you will do, what you are going to write. Going to. It is not here–now, but in the future. You try to see the "texts of the future".

Is that bad then?

No. But when you think, you only hear yourself. I'm trying to help you, but you are so preoccupied with your own thoughts that you are not receiving the signals. You are like Archimedes.

?

He worked day and night trying to solve his "problem". He was so intensely preoccupied with his own thinking, that it was impossible for me to help him see what he was looking for. After being exhausted, he actually gave up. He went to relax and take a bath.

And then?

Then he saw what I was trying to say. The water ran over, and he ran naked through the streets shouting EUREKA!! He stopped thinking and bingo! - he saw what I had been trying to show him for a long time. But he was not open to it until he gave up. He was in his own thoughts.

Please continue...

Thoughts are a way of placing an order. You pick up your order by ceasing to think.

Brilliant!

That's the recipe for brilliance, yes.

ABOUT GENIUS

If you do not see everything as genius, you can not see genius in anything. You see, the ingenuity lies in the connection between all things. That is where you have to look to see everything. The funny thing with this, is that you already use this method when you say that you "prove" something. You show that it is confirmed by a number of other "factors", implying that whatever your theory is, is confirmed by that other "fact".

At the same time, you overlook the very fact that "proof" isn t really "proof" until you can see the connection with everything. Since what you try to describe is a part of life- everything is- then nothing is actually "proven" until everything is. If you cannot see the connection with all there is, NOTHING is what is proven.

At one time, you started to make this easier for yourselves. You invented "scientific proof", which really is no more than easing the requirements for proof. Instead of looking for the connection in relation with everything- seeing whatever it is that you look at in the context of life itself- you now just need "scientific evidence" to prove anything. Which is, simply put, to claim that it does not need the connection with everything. Suddenly you need just limited proof, and then and there you invent the term "scientific proof".

What is now to become visible to you, is that what you have done, is to only prove your theories within a theoretical context that is only a little bit bigger. As an example- your theories about human beings are, at present, just about human beings. As if humans are not part of nature, but rather a separate being in itself. So your questions become limited. You do not seek life in itself anymore, you look for the "reality" of humans as a separate entity.

You split up "reality" into smaller parts. And what happens, is that reality becomes relative. Reality becomes different "topics". And you see the different parts not related to the whole, but only related to itself. It is like "knowing" the human body by knowing all the different parts separately. So you start believing that you can know parts of life without life as a context.

You will soon see that whatever is not naturally a part of everything, is only an answer to nothing.
Einstein had this thought. He saw that what was needed to create science with real "proof", was to find the formula describing the movement of life itself. That is what he tried to find with his "Theory of Relativity". His question was simply: "How is everything connected?"

He wanted to see the movement of the universe. "I want to know the thoughts of God", he said. He thought that I have thoughts. He thought that God thinks about what God is. Therefore he did not quite get there. But he was close. Had he been able to overcome his own question, he would have seen that there are no answers. You do not need to find the answer to anything. When life is the question, the

123

answer is always the same. Everything IS. There is no why in it. The answer to everything is not. Only everything IS.

His question, though, implied answer. But what is the answer to nature? What is the answer that has room for grass, trees, rabbits, planets and human beings? Nothing. Nothing is what holds everything. The search for answers is the movement towards limiting life, when life is the opposite movement. Life is the movement of the unlimited. The only true thing about life is that it is limitless. Life is the movement towards nothing. It is like everything is expanding, and its unreachable goal is to fill all the nothing there is. Endless, this journey is. No answer is the answer to everything. No answer is the answer to nothing. A straw of grass IS. It has no answer. But as soon as you see life in the grass, you see the movement of life. That is the only answer: Witnessing life in experience, not capturing life in knowledge.

Everything is evidence of the existence of everything. The only thing that can ever be proved is your experience. So ask. With no understanding. Then you, also, enter the limitless. Your true nature.

CONVERSATION WITH MY DECEASED MOTHER

I would like to talk to my mother. I need to tell her something.

Go ahead – she is here.

I am here, and I know what you want to say.

Yes, I'm sorry that I wasn't there. When you "died".

Apology accepted. Not because I need it, but because you need it, my son.

Yes, I needed to say it.

I know.

Are you alright?

Yes, I really am.

I've heard that you work in the "City of Lights"?

Yes. I did. But now I miss the physical life. That's just how it is.

So you will be coming back soon?

I think so.

Maybe you're already here? I've had a feeling.

Maybe.

Hmm. Good to have said it.

It's good that you say it. Good for you. You need it. And I have to say; it's quite a task you've taken on. But everything else would be too small for you, Jon. You've always been like that. Just so you know, your dad and I didn't make it easy for you to be you. I/we didn't see it at the time, but we were actually jealous of you. You could, or can, do anything. We never wanted anything but the best for you. And that was what we thought we gave you. And I guess we did, really. If you could see it from here, you would see so yourself. We were the tools that created the change you've been through, and are in the middle of.

I love you, Mum. And I miss you.

I love you, too, Jon. And I'm insanely proud of you.

Thanks.

Jons Bok 1 (en.)

Thank you. Dad sends his love.

HOLY ACT

Hello. Are you there?

Yes.

I want to ask you about christening S.

Ok. What about that?

As you know, we struggle a bit with finding the best solution.

Yes. I know. I see that as a good thing. That means you don't take it lightly.

Well, yes. It has to feel right. We want it to be about our values and so on- you know what I mean. At the same time, I would like the ceremony to have a feeling of importance, or holiness. I want it to be a sacred act.

Anyone taking this matter as seriously as you do, makes it a sacred act.

Yes. But I need to know the purpose of christening.

There is none.

There IS none!?! What do you mean?

*If a priest says ten thousand "Holy words" over your daughter, and it means nothing to **you**, it will have no value whatsoever.*

Whatever action you take, because you believe in it from the bottom of your heart, is a sacred act.

But, if you get the Pope himself to do this for you, and it means nothing to you, it will not be sacred at all.

As you know, where you go to find the God in you – me – is inside yourself. So any act you go through with, without your approval from your own deep inside, will not be connected to God. It will therefore not be a sacred act. There are no one else than yourselves that can add holiness to anything. Period.

So if I say "Welcome to this world. I will treat you to the best of my knowledge", and MEAN it, it will be a more "HOLY" christening than if a priest does it by the book?

Of course. Indeed.

But don't you have any suggestions as to what would be important to have as part of the
ceremony?

Of course I have. But does that matter?

Yes.

No. It does not. What matters, is what is important to you.

M-m...

In a Christian christening, what happens, is that the parents and a few other people, take solemn oaths that they will see to it that the child will get a Christian upbringing. But most of them don't mean it. What is that?

Lying?

Yes. And it would be an act that is not sacred for the parents, nor the child. In addition to the lying.
One could make a lot of jokes about people seeing that as "giving the child a good start in life"...

But Jesus did christen people, did he not?

*I promise you: That was **VERY** different from how it is done today. When Jesus christened people, he made them state publicly WHAT THEY THEMSELVES BELIEVED IN.*

And Jesus also knew a lot more about who I am, and WHAT I am, than the priests you are considering using in your ceremony. The ceremonies they used then, were based on the TRUTH. The ceremony they use now, is built on a very twisted truth. A truth that has been changed to serve someone else's purpose. That is the COMPLETE OPPOSITE of what Jesus did.

Yes. I can see that. But I don't see the ceremony being "sanctimonious" if we perform this ceremony ourselves.

Why not?! As I have just told you; how "holy" an act is, does not depend upon WHO is performing it. It depends on a TRUE INTENTION of commitment to the promises made. And also a commitment to do what is in the child's best interest.

So, if you could vote on this, your vote would go to us doing this ourselves?

No. It would go to you doing whatever makes you feel that you give to your daughter an HONEST PLATFORM to build her life on. And that you commit to stay on that path. As truth changes, so do you. And as a parent, you could do what you can to help your child live HER truth.

Ok. It does not matter WHO does it. But it has to be TRUE for us? And we make promises we can keep. That's just about it?

I think that would give your daughter "a good start in life", yes. Start building on REALITY from the very beginning. Don't you agree?

Yes. I do. Thank you.

Jon Schau

You are so welcome. Thank you for asking. I think it is a sign of maturity and adulthood that you come here to ask.

Thank you

Thank YOU.

Jon Schau

You are so welcome. Thank you for asking. I think it is a sign of maturity and adulthood that you come here to ask.

Thank you

Thank YOU.

WELCOME TO BE A PLAYER

Hello. Are you there?

Yes.

Is it as simple as it says in this book I am reading; decide that you are healthy, and then you are?

Yes. You have asked me this before. Try it. You do not need to try to understand it intellectually anymore. That is your way – to use your brain. You are satisfied with understanding mentally. Stop that right now. It is a form of escape. Instead of incorporating your knowledge into your being, you busy yourself with theoretical mind games. You don't need that anymore. You know ALL THERE is to know. You always have. But you haven't BEEN any of it.

And, in essence, spirituality is not about theoretical understanding; it is about BEING your understanding. You can understand everything – in fact, you do - but it gives you nothing – NOTHING – if you cannot BE what you know.

Ok. I need to focus on that. I understand.

133

Jon Schau

Yes. You understand. Same old, same old. This has nothing to do with understanding, though. It is, again, about BEING.

A sport you know well, is soccer. Look at the crowds going to see a game. They stand there UNDERSTANDING all of it. Most of them even feel they understand it BETTER than the players and their coaches. They all know how this is done, or should be done. But the plain truth is: THEY ARE SPECTATORS. They don't participate. They are watching others, and they comment on it. But the ones MAKING SOCCER HAPPEN, are the ones out on the pitch. You need to MAKE LIFE HAPPEN. Get out on the playing field. You are NOT supposed to be a spectator. You can be a PLAYER, right now. Are you up to it?

You have really caught me off guard right now. All I can say now, is this: I want to be.

Well. That is a start. The place where all players come from. But you need to decide: Do you want to play?

Yes. I want to. You have really given me a slap on the wrist now. You have opened my eyes. It is the truth about me. I am a spectator. Or, I have been, up until now. It has even been my job. To watch, and to comment on what I see. I need to take it one step further. I see that now. Thank you.

You are welcome. Welcome to be a player.

134

UNEASE AND HONESTY

Thank you for bringing more interesting people into my life. It really helps me to believe that change is possible.

Well, it is not "bringing more interesting people" that makes change possible. It is your desire to change that creates meeting people who can help. Do not surrender your power over your own experience. Not to me, nor to "interesting" people. You create, not I.

Except, you do.

Well.. Of course.

Do you think that my books are part of the reason for the unease that I feel?

They are the very core of that unease. The books are you being honest about who you are. And it is, in fact, the only thing you can contribute in this world. That you live as yourself, and share the experience you really have. Everything else is, at best, old news that you spread further. It has already been brought into the world by

135

Jon Schau

others. Otherwise, you could not have learned it. It could not have buzzed around in your thoughts.

So, why is it a bit uncomfortable for me then?

Because you are taking a risk. A real risk. And you are not used to it. Not in this way – exposing the real you. It is not strange that you have to think twice. See it as a positive sign. A sign that you have matured. You are worried about not doing the right thing. Not for others, but for you. You are quite used to doing what is right for them. But, it is a relatively new experience doing something that is right for you.

Well, I've been honest during my last two performances...

It is not about being honest. It has to do with what it is you are honest about. Everyone can be honest about what the time is. It is about not failing to be honest about yourself. Being honest does not necessarily mean you tell people about yourself. There is a big difference.

Yes, I get that. But feeling a little uneasy at the thought is quite normal, I suppose?

Yes. It is nothing to worry about. That's how it is. You will quickly get over it. Because, deep inside you, it feels good, doesn't it?

Yes. It does. I admit it.

Don't admit anything. When you are honest about yourself, there is nothing to admit. Do you not see that?

Yes. I see it. Mister Know-it-all.

TO BE LEARNED FROM ADOLF HITLER

Ok. I am ready. I have been postponing this conversation because I have this feeling it could be very provocative to many people. But here we go- I am ready now. You want to talk about Adolf Hitler?

Yes. I do. You know, people has this tendency to extract knowledge and understanding from the "good" experiences in life. But many find it so important to distance themselves from "evil", that they just do not look close enough to extract the same amount of understanding. Therefore, often the message has to be given in another way.

Hey, hold on! Are you not now saying that evil recreates itself because people do not *get it?*

Yes, I am. Very observant. It is what is often referred to as "bad karma". The "evil" is just as much trying to show you something as "good" is. But since people often choose not to look at "evil", it has to reproduce. Because- the ORDER HAS BEEN PLACED. The order for that which can be seen from it.

138

So, I take it- you want to tell me something that we did not *get* from Hitler? Something which is there to learn from it, which we did not see?

Exactly. And it is important. Because that which you have not yet seen, is the very thing that is to be learnt from it.

Are you saying we learnt nothing from Hitler?

In essence- yes. You have not yet seen that which is to be seen.

Wow. I am actually a little nervous now...

No reason to be.

Ok.I trust you, of course. Let´s hear it.

He said, reluctantly..

Yes. It is such a potent angry- maker, this.

You have all distanced yourself from Hitler. You have been detoured to believe that that which is to be learnt from Adolf Hitler, is to say NO to everything he stood for.

Yes..?

What DID he stand for? The IT that you distance yourself from- what IS it?

Hmmm... Being evil?

Jon Schau

And that is the big nothing that you have learnt from it.

Is that nothing? To choose love before hate?

Now you are saying that the IT was hate..

Yes. I am.

What created the hate? What is making the hate? The very thing that made this replicate into so many people? I am sure you agree that there are still individuals that carry hate inside of them? So- what is it that turned into such a widespread disease?

I don t know... (My mouth is open..)

In one word...

YES....?

CONCEPTUALIZATION.

What!?!?!

The Conceptualization of humans and life itself. You see- as long as humans believe that life is a concept, you can turn them into whatever you want. You can tell them that they hate Jews, and they will. You can tell them that fish tastes bad, and they will think it does. You can tell them that medicine is the way out of depression, and they will believe you.

Why?

140

Because: If life is a concept, you can suddenly do it well. Or bad. You can be judged. People can tell you whether you are good or not. Other people get to judge you.

And?

You start caring about their judgment. You will, after just a short while, start believing their judgment. Then- their judgment of you, is the You that you see. So, if they say that you are bad when you do this, or good when you do that- you start choosing to do that which they judge to be good. You are now soon to be totally enslaved by their definition of you. You start doing "good", and not doing "bad".

I see what you are getting at. But- is that really a problem? People doing "good"?

The problem is that what others judge as "good", might be "evil" to you. But you let others decide for you. So you think that you are doing "good" when people tell you so. Instead of accessing your emotional Self. Your Angel, your Creativeness. Which could, actually, tell you the exact opposite. I say to you: There are no human beings, when accessing their emotional experience, that will agree to putting other people at harm. They will instead start saying things like: "There is nothing in me that will ever do that to another human being".

How can you say that so bombastically? That no person can, when asking himself, be made to do anything evil?

Because- asking herself, is accessing her emotions, her Self. And THAT, my dear, is ME. Your emotions are my language. It is

141

where I speak. And also- do you notice the word you suddenly use?
"Be made to do"? Isn t that revealing? Suddenly you ARE not evil-
you are not even DOING evil! Suddenly you use the term being
MADE to do. You see it. You are starting to talk like me.

Hmm..

Don t you see the impossibility in what you said? "...when asking
himself, be made to.." Either you ask yourself, or you are being made
to. So you are saying the exact same thing as I am. IF you ask
yourself, you cannot be made to do anything. If you, on the other
hand, do not ask yourself- you can be made to do anything. ANY
THING. That is what I am also saying here. You just used other
words.

I am lost for words right now. I have nothing to say. I
just- agree.. But it is shaking me up a little. Stirring me.

Why?

The totally honest version? I have problems believing
that it is that simple. That it is so perfect.

I have, since we started these conversations of yours, been saying
this over and over again: It IS perfect. And when you see it, you will
be AMAZED by its simplicity. That is the sheer beauty of this. It is
so simple. Because it is Your Natural Way of Being. You just have
to be You.
And all is well.

INSANITY

There's something I've been thinking about – does insanity exist? Can a person go mad?

No. It is not possible to go mad. It is only possible for the outside world to define a person as mad.

Hmm. That's really interesting. Why are so many people afraid of going mad then?

Their egos are afraid of not being important anymore. Afraid of not being listened to.

But isn't that actually worse than being mad?

If you think you are dependent upon being listened to, then yes. But you actually don't need it.

Ok, well – but isn't associating with other people partly what life is about?

Jon Schau

Why do you think that?

I don't know. It just feels like everything would be wasted then. Not being able to share your life experiences with anyone...

But, you see, you always share this with everyone. "Life lives you", remember? In that way, your experience is accessible to life itself, which again is EVERYTHING. There is nothing else but this one life. There is nothing that is not a part of life.

Life is incredible, I have to say.

I am happy that you can see that.

WHAT GOD IS

God is a force. Or God is the material from which you create. The empty room you need in order to make something completely new. The void that has room enough for the entire creation that is you.

You can choose to make use of this force, or material, for anything you want. You can think of it as a tool to satisfy your ego, or you can see it as your task to make this force visible to others. You are free to do with it as you please.

With no effort nor any regret, you can do exactly what you want with God. That is why God is Nothing. Because it can build EVERYTHING. It has no limits.

So, knowing God has nothing to do with knowing God's will. Because it does not exist. To know this force, is to be aware of what you create. It is, in fact, knowing that you create. Becoming aware of creation.

When you see that you are the creator, then there is no one or no thing to blame. There is no wrong, no right. Only nothing. And this nothing is your framework for life. To know creation is to know God. The universe is yours. For you are God.

Now – be that.

CONCEPTUALIZATION

In many areas of the world, the conceptualization of life is preferred. The observation of life
is the objective.

Instead of the experiencing of it.

In this lies the key
to both the complexity and the simplicity of life.

In the Concept of Life are the comparisons, the definitions and the expectations.
In the Experience lies whatever you want.

If you close your eyes in a prison cell, you can be where you want.
If you are in the Concept of Life instead of the Experience, you are imprisoned by all circumstances.

EVOLUTION

Do you feel the Urge? The Force that is always there? Always wanting. Eager. Willing. Moving. Do you FEEL it?

THAT is inspiration. It is the GOD force. The driving force of Evolution. The MAKER of Universes!
Do you FEEL it? Living. Pumping. Inside you?

Then USE it. Create that which the force is telling you. Make into reality those DREAMS that are powered by the Urge. Plunge into Evolution.

This force is what is making you feel restless. Restlessness is Unfulfilled Dreams waiting to come alive. Dreams that are untouched by your creative force.

Do you know what happens when you do not see it? When you do not know what is causing your restlessness?

You start blaming LIFE. You are trying to fulfill the Urge, but instead- since you do not see your own dreams- you blame the situation that you are in. The conditions around you become the cause of your restlessness. NOW is not good enough. You want to try ANOTHER NOW. You THINK.

But what it is, is the unfulfilled Creative Force telling you that it is time for you to do what you are meant to do: LIVE YOUR DREAMS. Your life is the dreams that you let become.

In this way, a missed payment, a broken leg, an angry co-worker, become that which is the cause of your feeling of not wanting to be here.

But it is not about what you do not want. it is about you not letting in that which you want.

So. Before you make fulfilling your dreams the very purpose of life, you will not find rest. Rest is not stillness. Rest is to be constantly refilled by the Flow of Life Energy while Evolving.

Because Evolution is: Your Dreams brought into Life.

INNER AND OUTER CHANGE

An enduring change is an inner change. One small inner change over time leads to huge changes in your perspective on the world.

A change in circumstances that does not reflect an inner change is never permanent.

The reason for this is that an inner change takes you closer to who you really are, while focus on outer change leads you further away from it.

THE MEANING OF WORDS

Sometimes I have problems keeping the process moving. I think it's difficult to find new things to ask you about all the time. Do you have any suggestions?

Do you think you need some?

Don't I?

Well, as I see it, you are in the process all the time. Constantly. The process is about more than coming up with new questions all the time.

Such as?

Wonder. Continue to seek. Not least, be interested. And in this way, you are admirably loyal to the process. You go inside with nearly everything. Only on rare occasions you go outside.

151

I agree with you, of course. But I still like writing these conversations down. That is probably what I am missing. Writing these conversations.

Well, I understand.

And that's why I feel I have to come up with new questions all the time. Because when I write, I need a subject. Otherwise, it becomes just words. Words without meaning.

Which is, of course, what words are. Words are without meaning. Words mean nothing. It is you who give the words meaning. So to have meaning, you don't need words. And that is what you think is difficult, putting meaning into words. You will, in fact, discover that this will become even more difficult. Because the closer you get to the truth, the more you will see that there are no words to describe it.

So, it is a good sign that I cannot seem to come up with new questions all the time?

Well, if you want to get closer to the truth, you could put it that way. But, that is up to you. If you see it as a good sign, then it's a good sign. For you.

And therefore also for you.

IT'S ABOUT YOU

If you take everything you feel that you are missing in your life and imagine that you have it. How would you have felt then?

You would have been uncomfortable with it. Because then you would have had to decide what you wanted to have.

If you did everything that you should do. If you did everything that would make your parents proud. How would it feel?

You would feel uncomfortable because then you would have to find out what you wanted to do.

ABOUT REALITY

People who call themselves realists are often the most un-realistic. Because they constantly ignore their own reality. If their own reality is impossible to prove, as in: confirmed by others, then they turn away from their own reality.

Which is completely un-realistic. To not trust in one's own reality – how realistic can it be?

CLIMATE CRISIS

What will be the solution to the climate challenges?

A good word: Challenges. They are definitely possible to solve. Everything is. What is happening now is very similar to what happens when people ignore the warnings their bodies give them. The situation escalates until you have heard it and acted on it.

So people will find a solution?

That is not what I said. What will happen is that nature will find a solution. It is that simple. Nature will find a solution. People can choose to work together with nature or against it. You know, that is all that has happened. People have gone against nature. No one can do that for long. You can't win over nature. It's a battle no one can win. Nature always wins.

You're nature, aren't you?

Yes. I am. I never lose. I do not win either. I am. Always.

155

But, in a way, so are we?

Of course. Life can never stop. Nature will always be there. Seen from nature's side, there is no danger at all. If humanity decides to become extinct, that is not a problem for life itself. It will continue regardless. No matter what people decide to do with themselves. For nature, this is not a big deal.

I can see that. But wouldn't it be a significant set-back - if the human race became extinct?

No. It wouldn't. We are all souls. It will always be like this. You know, many people die every day.
Do you notice anything in particular when that happens?

Well, no.

Exactly. All people die. People are not really people. You are energy. Eternal. You will always exist. Just like me, in fact.

Hmmm. Are there really no problems?

Not really, no.

But do you really think that we should just sit back and watch this, and not do anything?

If that's what you decide. If you do not see a reason for doing anything about it.

Why?

Nature does not need anything. Not even people. You are not THAT important. Remember, the worst that can happen is that life changes form. That's all.

But then we would not have this stage to play on anymore, to experience life?

When you died, did you stop experiencing things?

No.

Well then. Nothing is ever lost. The worst imaginable scenario is that you change form and become a part of nature, a part of life again. You will perceive or experience yourselves as a part of nature once more.

Hmm. This is really making me think.

If it worked like this on everybody, wouldn't that be great?

Yes. Probably.

There. You see? This is actually not as big a deal as you all think.

This is more than enough for me to grapple with for a day or two. Thank you. I think.

Don't worry. Nature will always exist. You are a part of nature. It is as simple as that.

Good night. I hope.

Jon Schau

Good night.

PEARLS FOR SWINE

Make other people feel like a resource.

That was you, right?

Yes. That is a very good start. If people learn to see themselves as resources, just think of the implications... If people don't, how can they really participate? How can you contribute, if you think you have nothing to give?

This is HUGE. I am thinking of all the people in the world that don't have a chance even to BEGIN to think of themselves in that way... It makes me SO SAD!

Yes, it is sad, isn't it? The greatest resource, actually the ONLY resource, you have, are HUMANS. But you don't seem to see that. You are wasting human resources to get to other resources (i.e. gold and money...). When the most valuable resource you have – BY FAR – are humans.

It is like spending millions of dollars on dirt almost...?

Jon Schau

Yes! You take one valuable resource in exchange for LESS of a much less valuable resource. That is total madness. But it is happening ALL THE TIME.

What is the matter with us!!??

You don't see yourselves as resources.

Hmmm. I am getting angry now. I am really outraged.

I am not, but I can understand how you feel.

We really need to change.

If you say so. I want to ask you something. If people saw what you are seeing, would they feel what you are feeling?

Of course! Or, at least I think so...?

So, make them see, then. If you want to change this.

Very good point.

This is the core of so many problems. People don't SEE. Because they don't LOOK.
This is very strange. If people could see themselves, they would change instantly. So there is no gap between what people want, and what they do. The gap is between what they see, and what they do.

It is all a matter of honesty. If people would look upon themselves with complete honesty, they would see. And as soon as they saw, they

160

would change what they do. Then people would start doing what they want. Seen from here, it is sometimes ridiculous how helpless people make themselves. They cannot even seem to do what they want!

And we think we are very developed as a race...

Yes. You do. And that is the cork in the bottle. You think you have come as far as you can go.

As we have through the centuries....

Yes. And what happens, is that you stop thinking about these matters. A person who thinks he knows everything, does not seek any more knowledge, does he?

No. Because you do not look for something you "know" to exist...

Exactly. You smile at your history, and learn nothing from it.

I have been thinking of this for a long time.

I have been with you for a long time.

He, he.... Kool!

:) :)

SEE ME IN EVERYONE

I'm back. No particular reason. I just want to stay in touch.

That is fine with me.

It is good to know you're always there. I like it a lot.

I cannot not be here, you know. Just like you. I am here. Forever. You cannot lose me. As I cannot lose you. We are forever the same.

I know. Still feels good, though.

I am glad you feel that way. It sure will make things a lot easier for you.

Yes. I see that. It always helps, these conversations we have. You are so spacious, so roomy. You have an answer for everything.

Through YOU. Remember that. You see, the one doing the most difficult thing here, is you. I talk to everyone. Only a few people manage to listen. So actually, YOU are the one standing out here. More than me.

Which is the same.

Yes.

I know I have to stay on track with what I'm supposed to do here. Or, I don't have to, but I want to.

Yes.

Is there anything I should know?

No.

Nothing?

You can never not be on the right track. So there is really no more I can tell you. You know all there is to know. All I know, you know, too.

This "we are all one", is so clear to me now. It is weird to think about it being so hard to understand, or GRASP, earlier. Now it is just so OBVIOUS. It cannot be any other way.

You still need to work on implementing it into your life, though. You understand it, but it is still not your instinct. When you look at something or someone, you see me. But it is not your automatic reaction. Yet. But it will be.

You are right. I don't see me in every other person I meet. I forget that all the time. I suppose that it is important for me to be able to what I want to do?

Yes. It is essential. Part of the "basic package" that needs to be in place.

I guess I could practice that?

Yes. Of course. Every single situation in your life is brought to you/ made BY you to see more of you, or remember more. Every single one. You can practice that.

Yes. But I cannot be on the alert ALL the time. I would be exhausted.

Would you, really? I have to disagree. You see - at present you need to concentrate to see reality.
When you get to where you are going, you will not need to concentrate. It will be an integral part of you. Like breathing. And you don't find that particularly exhausting, do you?

No. I don't. And of course you're right.

Just a suggestion: Practice more often. You are really very close. It does not take much effort for you to get here. If you think about it, haven't you noticed that you are here when you speak to other people about life and how you see it? It just comes to you naturally. Because you have focus. Try and put the same focus into it when you look around you, also.

I will. But somehow I don't find that easy.

It will become easy. It could be part of your way of viewing the world tomorrow already. You are THAT close.

As I said, I'll try. I will make an effort to get there. By the way, popping up in my mind right now is the feeling that I have to remove the fear of being independent to be able to get there.

Yes.

That is true, is it not?

When you were younger, you did not have that fear. You were, if you think back, quite fearless. There was no challenge you wouldn't take. Then, because of your losses, that fear rose in you. You were not invulnerable anymore. You will need to get back to that state of mind.

I see. Any suggestions?

LOOK AROUND YOU.

Ok?

You have faced a lot of uncomfortable situations lately, have you not?

Well, yes...?

Jon Schau

And they are all related to your discomfort of being dependent on others. Is it not obvious what you are trying to show yourself? The sense of security you seek, is not to be found in that direction. You can search for as long as you like, but that is not where you will find it.

What you have done, in plain language, is to make sure you have a back exit, a way out. If things get too tough to handle, you can exit there.

You have made it easy for yourself to find excuses if things should go wrong.

Very close to you, in the background, you have made sure you have a ticking bomb. And if you needed it you could set it off. You could, at any given time, become a victim of illness. There has always been some way out. And you see, when you create things with that in mind, you cannot really be successful. And deep down that is what you really want.

What we have been doing since your stay in the hospital, is building your character from scratch. Now you know who you are. What you are here to do. That is all you need to feel safe. You can start creating without that back door. And it is very, very important that that is what you do when you make your comeback. YOU DON'T NEED A SAFETY NET! So don't create one. Trust yourself. Trust me. Now we will go all the way. And in our plan there is no escape route. Now people will see the REAL you. With all of your potential. And, Jon, that is HUGE! You have NO IDEA!

Actually I see your point. I see what you mean with that safety net. In some strange way, it has come to that: I feel

166

safer if things could go wrong. Because then people would feel "sorry" for me, and help me if things should go wrong.

Yes. That is exactly what I am talking about. But now you don't need that anymore.

No. I don't. I have you. And I have my own family now. It's time to enter the arena, putting everything on the line. Because there really is nothing to lose anyway.

Now you're seeing it. And NOW, FINALLY, you see why you needed to be ill for so long. And – by seeing that – IT WILL BE GONE. Jon, you are now as healthy as you ever were. You are ready. You are REALLY, REALLY ready now.

Nice timing, I must say, 2 months before the baby arrives.

Don't you think? Now, let's get down to business.
You have, even with all the problems I have told you about, always been a force to reckon with. From now on it will be incredibly stronger. What we are building here, through you, is a force so strong it cannot be overseen. We are about to change the way people look upon themselves and the world around them.
What we're about to unleash on people, they have never experienced before. Be AWARE of that. There will be people fearing this. It is not going to be easy all the time. But now you've found the ground to stand on. You are firm. AND: You are right.
The truth is always what people want. Even though they don't even know it themselves.

Jon Schau

I feel a little, tiny bit scared. But most of all I am very inspired. I feel awfully strong right now!!

You are. You are ready. You are strong. And you are helping a lot of people with what you are about to do. What WE are about to do. Now, go sleep. Tomorrow, we will start. NOW IT IS TIME. WE ARE READY NOW.

GIVE AND RECEIVE. BALANCE.

(This started while I was out swimming.)
Ok, ok. To sum it up: I need to see everything as ONE?

Yes. Everything you give and everything you get is part of the universe. And when you give something, you get it back. But not always from where you think. Because the universe is one, you can get back what you give from somewhere else than where you gave it.

Example?

D's parents. You give there. You get from Anna and your friends. It is all the same.

So then people misunderstand this whole thing. Because it is always the whole ONE giving and receiving from itself at the same time. And, as being part of that one, I give and receive at the same time. To me that sounds like what you mean is giving and receiving is only to keep the balance in the whole, in the ONE. Which is you.

That is ABSOLUTELY CORRECT. You see it! Very good!

And then suddenly I see why competition is such a ridiculous concept. It just helps keep the imbalance in place. Giving and receiving is the CORE of the universe s ability to restore itself, in order to keep the universe in balance.

Yes. But remember that the universe does not rely on you humans. The universe takes care of itself. When an imbalance is too big, it restores the balance itself.

You're saying we better look out?

This has nothing to do with fear. You will also gain from a balanced universe. Actually, if it wasn't like that, the Christians could be right: That you humans are just a nuisance, a mistake. But you're not. You are part of the universe. As is everything.
What the future of the universe is, nobody knows. Not even I. It is always evolving. My point here is that if everyone does their part to keep the balance, the universe would evolve much faster. It would not have to spend time restoring balance all the time.

What you just said has enormous implications . It means that people being afraid/ having fear are, in reality, afraid of themselves. So to free yourself from fear, the recipy seems to be to get to KNOW yourself. To see that there is nothing to be afraid of?

What are psychologists trying to do all the time?

They are trying to make people see their lives as they really are?

In a perfect world, yes. But most people don't know where to look to find themselves. Psychologists included. Doctors included. Politicians included.

So what is lacking – the ONE thing that would solve ALL problems, is that people see themselves as they are. And therefore see YOU?

Salvation. You just described salvation. I even think you gave a very clear picture.

Thank you. For making me see.

Thank you. For making me experience seeing.

Back to the balance we talked about before. Restoring that balance is part of my mission, is it not?

Yes. It is. But you are not alone.

I know. I figured that one out myself. I want to ask you straight out, since I find these conversations so important. Should I not share this with people? Am I really meant to keep all this to myself?

Of course NOT. It is just a question about how to get the message through. Most people are not ready for what you have been experiencing. What you are writing right now, would make no sense to you just one year ago.

Jon Schau

Think back to what started this for you. You got that book from "nowhere". That was all it took. You needed to be inspired.

And I know no person that has the ability to inspire people like you. That is your vision: To inspire people to start searching. Because they all have different paths. They just need to be inspired to start. THAT is your job. You can say it like this: Jesus came to show what people really are. Your job is to inspire them to start looking, so that they SEE what Jesus really tried to tell them.

Now I understand that bond I have been feeling with Jesus.

Yes. Now you know what needs to be done. But remember this: Do not preach anything. Show them what happens when you find the light. Be that light.

This could have some pretty big implications?

Yes. It's about time. You (humans) are really slow these days. You have been so caught up in all the "wrong" things. Now it's time to restore the balance. To show people what they really are. To save the world.

It is clear to me now. I am able to see everything as one. At least a lot of the time. I feels most difficult when I am alone, actually.

I want to tell you a secret: It was exactly the same with Jesus. He had the same problem. I think that it is easier to "be there" with

172

other people around you. Because how can you really see yourself in others, when there's no one else around? You should not worry about it. So, my point: No one, not even Jesus, managed to do what you're trying to. So don't be too hard on yourself about it.

As you know, Jesus was not "perfect" either. No one is, because: What is perfect? So don't try to be you. Be you. It worked for Jesus. It will work for you also.

Thank you so much.

–

Ok – here's more. So I am not going to teach anything? Not tell anyone about this – just SHOW THE EFFECTS?

YES!!! Because the effects are what people are after. Rich, poor, man, woman – the effects of seeing their own greatness is what they are looking for. Why do you think people want to be rich? Because they think that it will bring them happiness. But it will not. Nor will anything else, but the things you and I know.

If you stop and think: Why do you think people want to be rich? Because Richard Branson has told them how to do it, or because they see the results of what he does?

The results, obviously.

Exactly. So what you need people to see, are the results of their beliefs. Do not tell them what you believe. Because what you believe

Jon Schau

is WRONG FOR THEM WHERE THEY ARE NOW. It will make no sense to them.

They need to see your fearlessness, your love, and what that brings you. Then that will inspire them to look for it in themselves. And that is what we want. That people find themselves. Not that they agree with you.

Yes! I am so glad! This really helps me to find some direction in this.

And not just this, Jon. There is more. But we will get back to that later. This is only the beginning. This is big. I couldn't possibly explain it to you. Actually it would be great risk in doing so. If you knew what's coming, it would be very difficult for you to stay in the NOW. We want you to be there all the time, you know. That is the only way to set this in motion

Yes. And I am not interested in anything about the future either, so.. _
I notice that I have difficulties finding questions, something to wonder about. It feels like I need to know right now. And the future is just "wrong", in a way. I am not interested in the future before I get there, sort of. This is not about fortune-telling. The future is there to be altered anyways, by just creating something else instead. So- I am a little frustrated right now. Which direction to look? Where do I find what I am supposed to do? Where do I start? Do I need to look? Can I just go ahead without looking first? In that case, where and with what?

174

Is this supposed to be a show, a book, a film or what? I honestly have problems with translating this, all that I have now experienced, to a stage or whatever...? Maybe I am looking to create a new form altogether? A new form of standup comedy? A new form of entertainment? Maybe art, for all I know? Is the important thing that I come from something else now? Is that the thing? That it has nothing to do with for whatsoever?

Is this supposed to be the start of giving instead of receiving? If so, how do I do that? Is it not, like, baked into the concept of performing, that you receive? Recognition? I am so in dire need of some sort of key. An aha- moment that kicks me in the right direction. That just pass by like an image that then sticks? A vision. I feel I

haven t seen IT yet. And that is what I think I need: An image in my head of what I want to do.

Giving instead of receiving. Ok, I get that, but how do one do that? How different is that going to be? How many of the experiences I have had are really possible to use in this project? Do I have to become new also, or do I still be me? How much of "old Jon" should I keep? Nothing? Everything?
As you probably realize, I need help.

I think you are doing great. What you are writing now, is clearly written by a person in development, in process. Ond it is exactly where you are supposed to be! The reason this shows up now, is that the process is to be adjusted into becoming the project. Up until now, the process has been about "Who am I? What am I?"

Now that you have one answer to that, it is only natural to start asking: "But what is it for?"

It is like this for everyone. Noone being in a process knows where it ends. Then you are out of it. What you are asking for, are answers that are outside of the process. Within the process, the answers do not exist. There, the answers are created as you go along.

I think you could easily feel joyful for being in this process. You have spent a lot of time and energy to get into it. Now you are there, in it. And that is where you want to be. Do you not see that?

Yes. I saw it in the middle of your monologue. I want to be where I am. But I also want to know that it leads somewhere. To me, it is not a goal to become a monk in a monastery for 20 years being in process. I want to make use of the process. I want to show people the way into process. How life-changing it can be. How exciting it is. How neccessary it is, to the individual and for all of us.

If you ask me, you have started answering your own questions already.

I have. I know that. And I also know that I am making things clearer for myself through these conversations.

Yes. As I have said before- you are here now.

Yes. I am. At the same time I am a comedian on sick leave, with no salary, having a child in 2 months. I guess you can see that that makes me a little impatient? I want to go somewhere with this!

I get that. But I see something that you obviously do not see: You are in the middle of a powerful transformation. Very fast you are approaching the end of these questions.

Ok. I get that. I also agree. But do you see my point also?

Yes. I do. No problem. And that could go for you as well- to have no problems with this. The difficult part is already over. What is left, is the easy part. Your mind is full of alternatives. You just need to make up your mind about what you choose to go for.

Not so long ago, the process was about you lacking alternatives, and wanting to see them. Now it is already as good as over. Regarding this first step, that is.

In your life it will never be over. If you don t want it to be. And you do not want that.

No. I do not want that. Thanks for talking with me. Looking forward to next time.

Love.

———

I d rather ask you straight forward: Do I need a manuscript?

Jon Schau

Those that are looking for security outside of themselves, need a manuscript. And in doing so, is blocking their connection with true creativity, with fear.

So- no?

So- no. You want to feel secure in your self. You want the direct contact with me.

And therefore it is so easy to talk to you, and so incredibly boring to work on a manuscript?

Sometimes you ask such leading questions, that I don t even need to answer.

Yes. I am just getting rid of my insecurities.

Ok, then it might be better if I just gave you the right recipy. Because what you just described, is
NOT.

Oh, no?

Yes.

Thanks?

You cannot be GIVEN the sense of security. You have to GIVE it. To those around you. Which is you.
You speak as if I am something outside of you, that can give you something. But I cannot. Because I am in - inside of- you. I am part

of you, you are part of me. Two sides to the same story. The sense of security can only be found within you. Give it to yourself.

And then I need to throw away everything that I used to believe in... Manuscript, being well prepared, and so on.

Yes. The manuscript and what you call well prepared are the false sense of security you have felt before. As Jesus said all the time: You need nothing but me. And in the 10 commandments: THou shalt have no other Gods but me.

The manuscript and "well prepared" are other Gods. You do not believe that Jon Schau is good enough as himself, so you have created this dependency on those things. Which actually are two different things.

The manuscript is something palpable to hang on to, because you do not trust yourself, trust me. "Well prepared" is to learn that script. In reality you are now more prepared than ever before. Because now you don t have access only to the limited manuscript. Now you know you. Enough to trust you instead of the script.

Tell me- what is more flexible, funny, present now- you or the manuscript? The manuscript contains only that which is in it. You contain the whole universe.

In that comparison the manuscript becomes quite tiny, yes..

Then transform all your experience, everything you have learnt, all the things you know about trusting the script, into trusting YOUR SELF.

That is what will turn this into something that is so much greater than anything you ever did before. Since the script this time is Jon Schau.

No matter how good a script writer you can cough up, she will never be able to write even one percent of that manuscript. Can you see that?

Yes, I see that.

Ok. Then we agree. Focus on whatever part of YOURSELF that you are insecure about. When you have figured that out, your manuscript is ready.

Ok, I m in. I trust you.

PLEASE DO!

Thank you so much for existing.

—

The point of communication is to bring people closer to each other. To let people see one another, and in that seeing themselves. It is supposed to be a tool for understanding. In many ways, people have made it into the opposite. When people do not communicate honestly, and by that I mean complete honesty, it does not contribute to understanding.

People so often say that which they believe that others want them to say. If you just stop and ponder that a little, you will see that this instead creates even more distance between people.

Because, what then really happens, is that people don t communicate reality as it is. If you are to evolve further, it has to be built on reality.

This is what life is about: To be an individual that takes part, sharing who he or she really is. There is no other way to contribute to the evolution of humankind, than to tell the truth as you see it. Your reality. No matter what it is.

To communicate just for the sake of communicating, is hiding reality. The effect turns into the opposite of what it is supposed to be. Actually, it is way better to not speak, than to speak something that is not your experience. Then you at least avoid making it harder for people to recognize you as you really are.

ABOUT PUBLISHING THE BOOK

I must admit it sounds very tempting to write a book. It feels as if it will give me another way of sharing. Do you like the idea?

I LOVE the idea! I think you should try and spread the message in as many ways as you possibly can. And it will challenge you in so many different ways. And that will be good for all of you. You get to spread your creativity, and that is always good.

My thoughts, exactly...

Of course.

Yes. I feel I have nothing more to learn. I feel so much more inclined to being creative, than to try to gain more knowledge. It will not get me any further, anyway. Except that it will, of course.

You sound exactly like me now. Have you noticed?

I AM you. Remember?!!

Yippee! You're here! I really look forward to your book. I have read
it, you know. It is simply marvelous!

Can you tell me what it is about? Or is that not smart?

I do not think that is wise. You see – I am the one writing that
book. But the part of me I am using to do it, is you. If I told you the
whole story, I would not use your abilities. And that would mean I
had no use for you and your specific talent. But I DO need that. It is
never going to be what it is supposed to be, if I take you out of the
making of this book. Or, actually, THESE BOOKS. There will be
more than one. Many more.

When? Can you say anything about that?

Sooner than you think. Much sooner.

Good. I like that..

Yes. You do. Because, deep down, you LOVE writing. And I
know you do not know it yet, but you do. It will be just as easy for
you as writing down these conversations. It will come to you,
effortlessly.

Sounds great to me!

I know. On that you have instinctively used the right method,
actually since you were born. You have always been called
"LUCKY", because things come so easily to you.

But people who say that don't see that they could do exactly the same? Had they only been LISTENING to themselves...?

Yes. You are so close to your core being now, that you understand everything.

Or nothing.

Or nothing. And I like your saying that. We both know why it is so important to keep that in mind. ALWAYS.

Yes. I love talking to you. As you know. But now I really should get some sleep.

Yes. You should. See you later.